My
Turn
to
Care

My Turn to Care

compiled and edited by
MARLENE BAGNULL

A JANET THOMA BOOK

THOMAS NELSON PUBLISHERS
Nashville • Atlanta • London • Vancouver

10/98 lad 8/21/98 - 4c

Published in Nashville, Tennessee, by Thomas Nelson, Inc., Publishers, and distributed in Canada by Word Communications, Ltd., Richmond, British Columbia, and in the United Kingdom by Word (UK), Ltd., Milton Keynes, England.

ISBN 0-7852-8077-4

Printed in the United States of America
2 3 4 5 6 — 99 98 97 96 95

Dedicated to my husband, Paul,
and to our children,
Sharon, Debbie, and Robbie,
who stood beside me
when it was my turn
to care for my mother
and
to the 108 men and women
who contributed to this book
and shared their struggles
and joys as they took their
turn to care for an
aging parent

CREDITS

ॐ
CONTENTS

PREFACE

For months, I wondered and worried. Something was wrong, terribly wrong, with my mother, but I didn't know what. When the doctor finally diagnosed a dementia similar to Alzheimer's, my first reaction was relief. At least now I knew what we were facing. But the more I learned about this illness, the more my relief turned to fear. How were we going to cope with an illness that destroys the ability to reason and remember—an illness where there is no hope outside of a miracle?

"Why, God?" I wept. "Why *my* mother? She's suffered so much already. These are supposed to be the good years, the golden years. Instead, You've seen fit to take her husband and now to allow her mind to be taken by this disease."

As the oldest child, it was my turn to care for my widowed mother the last four and a half years of her life. During those years, I wept, not just for her, but for myself. I agonized over the ways Mother's illness affected our relationship. The child in me who still needed parenting was now required to do the parenting.

"Why, God? Why me?" I wept and sometimes grumbled as I struggled to meet the needs of my growing children, the demands of my growing career, and my mother's growing need for mothering. As much as I loved her, it was hard not to resent her. I didn't have the patience of a saint, or the wings of an eagle to rise above the pain of watching her deteriorate.

When it became obvious Mother could no longer live alone, my husband and I did a lot of talking and praying. We sought counsel from others. Finally, along with our two teenagers, we concluded she needed to come live with us. Little did we know what we were getting into or just how much she would disrupt our lives.

Mother didn't sleep at night. She rarely stopped complaining and lecturing during the day. My husband and son learned to tune her out or escape to another room, but my daughter got into arguments with her constantly. I was not a good referee!

As Mom's illness progressed, she became increasingly difficult, demanding, and manipulative. She required twenty-four-hour care. Exhausted, and torn between her needs and the needs of my family, I often felt I was failing everyone. And I felt angry—with my mother, with myself for not coping better, and even angry with God.

"Look for the hidden blessings, child," the Lord said to me more than once.

"Blessings?" I questioned. But they really were there when I chose to look for them. I caught glimpses of the mother I once knew. I began to see ways God was at work in both our lives. I saw the Lord deepening my relationship with Him and with my husband. And, I experienced God's strength in a new way when I had to put Mom in a nursing home and several months later when I had to release her into His hands and allow Him to take her through the valley of the shadow.

God's blessings will be different for each of us when it is our turn to care for an aging parent. Some may be clearly visible. Others we may see and understand only years later, perhaps not until we meet Him face to face. But this I know—even if we continue to badger Him with our "Why, God?" questions, even if we push Him aside when we most need Him, and even if "we are too weak to have any faith left" he will not abandon us (see 2 Tim. 2:13 TLB). He will minister to each of us, and to our loved one, in special and unique ways.

I pray God will use my experiences, and the experiences of those who have contributed to this book, to encourage you to look for His hidden blessings as you care for your aging parent. May you discover, as we have, that God is faithful and that He always keeps His promises.

G R O W I N G

O L D E R

Gray
hair is
a crown
of splendor;
it is attained by
a righteous life.

Proverbs 16:31 NIV

When I was a child, time seemed to drag. "When are we going to get there?" I'd ask my parents ten minutes after we pulled away from the curb.

"She's starting already?" Dad groaned.

"Shush and enjoy the ride," Mom pleaded.

But I didn't enjoy the ride! Why did it have to take so long to get there? And why did it have to take so long to grow up so I could wear lipstick and date like my cousin who lived next door?

Then suddenly it seemed as if someone pushed the accelerator after I got married and started having babies. Why did they have to grow so fast? Why did the days have to whiz by? I scarcely had time to grab the camera and capture their first steps and their first day in school.

Two of my children are now grown. My "baby" is taller than his father. Soon he leaves for college.

Time doesn't stand still! The 86,400 seconds that make up a day do seem to tick by more quickly the older we get. And as I've watched myself and my children grow older, I've seen the effect of time on my parents and on my husband's parents.

My mother and stepfather have already gone home to the Lord. I don't know how much longer we will have my husband's parents. Their gray hair is a crown of splendor and a reminder to value the time we have with them. Even though I often feel overwhelmed by my demanding schedule, I am determined not to miss spending time with them. These years of growing older together can be golden years for them—and for us. How?

Focus on the positives. Instead of dwelling on ways your parents may be starting to lose ground physically and mentally, rejoice for what they are still able to do. "Think about all you can praise God for and be glad about . . . and the God of peace will be with you" (Phil. 4:8–9 TLB).

Don't forget to give them encouragement and praise. Everyone needs encouragement and affirmation. Aging parents are no exception. Even if Mom's homemade pie isn't as good as it used to be, or if Dad's garden isn't as green, praise their efforts and let them know you appreciate them.

Do things together. Aging parents do not fit into busy to-do lists any more than growing children do, but it is worth rearranging your schedule for them. Like Pauline Youd, you may decide to make Wednesday Mother's day (see p. 39). Or maybe your parents live a thousand miles away and you'll need to plan vacation times to visit. Do everything possible to show them they are high on your priority list. Time is one of the most precious gifts you can give to them—and to yourself!

MOM'S NOT

DOING EIGHTY

Age should speak, and multitude
of years should teach wisdom.
—Job 32:7 NKJV

During my teen years, we called her Lead-foot Lucy. Mom would hop in her pink-and-white Rambler, zoom away from the curb, and race down the highway to her evening nursing job at the infirmary. I never worried about her then.

My dad always took care of so many things when he was alive, not giving Mom much independence. But one thing he did do was teach her to drive. It was not the prevailing attitude of men back then. I well remember one of my uncles saying, "No woman is ever going to drive my car."

From the number of women Mom picks up when she goes away, it's obvious other men were of the same opinion. But she learned to drive and in turn taught four children how to drive too.

Mom turned eighty this year. Now she's asking us if she should give up driving. It's not easy to make that decision for the person who taught you how to drive. I have mixed feelings about it, too, because I know how much Mom enjoys being out and doing. Although she drives more slowly than she once did, I know how impatient and reckless other drivers are.

This morning I talked with her on the phone. She wondered if I'd go with her to the doctor. His office is twenty miles away. At one time Mom thought nothing of driving alone for 200- or 800-mile trips to visit her children in Wisconsin and New York. Maybe she's making her own choice about driving. I wonder if I'll know when it's my time to stop?

Dear heavenly Father, teach us all to number our days that we may apply our hearts to wisdom.

—**Kathy Scott**

VIOLETS ARE
FOR REMEMBERING

*"Do not lay up for yourselves treasures on earth, . . .
but lay up for yourselves treasures in heaven. . . . For
where your treasure is, there your heart will be also."*
—Matthew 6:19–21 NKJV

My mother lives three states away. As she gets older, I
find myself hoarding her letters and savoring our phone
conversations hoping to capture those memories so I can
clutch them to my heart forever. Even though I know her
times, like my own, are in His hands, I am sometimes
fearful. I know these days will not last and, at some point,
I may have to go on living without her. Already Mom sends
a check and I do her Christmas shopping for me and my
family. She frets that it isn't personal enough but also
expresses relief.

This year I found myself steering clear of the usual
practical gifts of clothing when selecting gifts from Mom.
Instead, I searched for things that were tangible and lasting—things we wouldn't grow out of or wear out too soon.
I chose a white china teapot for myself. It's covered in
delicately painted violets, the flower of sentiment and

memory. I use it often and always think of Mom, so far away. I'm glad to have this physical reminder of her.

The other day Mom and I were chatting long distance. I complained about a volunteer project I had committed to doing. The work was not strenuous or difficult, but I couldn't seem to get along with the woman in charge. I dreaded going in to work and always left feeling incompetent.

Mom listened and without hesitating offered, "Would they let me come and do it for you?"

I gasped. "No, Mom!" And then I had to laugh as I pictured my silver-haired mother traveling nearly 500 miles to do a job I'd volunteered to do. How like Mom that is! Ready and eager to take my pain and do all she can to help me. How like our Lord too.

"Well," Mom continued, "if you won't let me do it, you'd better do something about it."

"What can I do?" I moaned. "She thinks I'm stupid and treats me that way!"

"You need to pray for that woman, Cathy."

I was stunned. "You're right," I confessed. "I've been too busy complaining and feeling like a martyr to pray for her."

As I hung up the phone and bowed my head, I thanked the Lord for the way my mother still gives me wonderful gifts—gifts more tangible and lasting than violet-covered teapots.

Lord, teach me to lay up treasures in heaven. Crystallize Your teachings in my heart and mind so I will not fear the future. Thank You for Your reminders that I am never alone.

—Cathy Jean Gohlke

R i s e   A b o v e

Lord, You've told me
   I shouldn't worry about anything
      but instead pray about everything.
You've told me that this is the secret
   to experiencing Your peace in the midst.
Yet today I forgot all about Your promises.
I grumbled instead of prayed.
I got up-tight and irritable,
   and took out on my loved ones
      that which I should have released to You.
Please forgive me, Lord.
I really blew it.
Lift me out of the pit of depression
   I have dug myself into.
Replace my negative feelings with positive ones—
   with the hope that comes from choosing
      to believe in You.
Help me to keep my eyes on You
   instead of circumstances.
Enable me to rise above

the things that frustrate and upset me.
Lord, I ask not that You change these situations,
but that You change my response to them
so that others may see You in me.

—**Marlene Bagnull**

A SIGNAL OF

CHANGING ROLES

There is a time for everything, . . .
a time to throw away.
—Ecclesiastes 3:1, 6 NIV

Once I'd finally admitted clutter addiction, I begged my daughter to visit to bring order into my life. Rolling up her sleeves, Robin asked, "Now, you're not going to get mad at me, are you?"

"No. I promise. Besides, I invited you."

She looked semi-convinced. "This won't be easy."

"But essential." I felt a twinge of panic. "Honey, I've tried to sort and throw out, but we're still inundated with . . . stuff." *Precious stuff*, I thought.

"There's nothing I can do about your papers. The books—"

"Mostly for school."

"But not all."

I sighed. "Not all." Many were titles I planned to read—sometime. After retirement. Or perhaps laid up with a broken leg . . .

"You know you won't."

I knew it. I lacked the necessary leisure . . . and commitment. Besides, there are libraries.

Next we unearthed caches of fabric and yarn. We filled bags for Goodwill and for the church quilters. We packed a box for my sister, who knits pincushions and Afghans.

Robin stretched. "Ready?"

She was eyeing my yard sale treasures.

I felt stirrings of defensiveness. "As long as I teach creative writing workshops . . . "

Incredulous, she pointed to my seashells, candle holders, geodes, metal sculptures, posters, baskets, sun catchers, ceramic figurines, plaques, milk glass. "You use *this*? For *creative writing*?"

"Not the milk glass."

"The rest?"

I nodded.

"How?" she challenged.

Rather weakly, I explained.

"When you quit teaching, you'll get rid of all of it?"

She waited.

I concentrated on my recent promise. "When I quit teaching," I mumbled.

"All right. Then here's how we'll reduce the rubble . . . "

Obediently, I clustered items in groups of ten, ranked in order of my attachment.

"Now," Robin directed, "fifty percent must go."

Choices became increasingly difficult. But Robin was persistent and I kept reminding myself that I had, out of desperation, invited this interference.

Although Robin and I struck a few sparks those four days, clutter diminished and my self-esteem improved. My thanks, as she prepared to leave, were sincere.

Robin called that evening to let me know she'd arrived safely. "I'm sorry, Mom," she whispered.

"Sorry! Why?"

She laughed self-consciously. "Halfway home I pulled to the berm and just sat there, shaking, thinking, *That was my mother I was bossing!*"

"Honey," I said, "your 'bossing' was just what I needed!"

As I hung up, tears stung my eyes. This had been our first experience in role reversal—her first taste of parenting her parent, my introduction to accepting discipline from my child. What a blessing we'd grown closer through the exchange!

Lord, thank You for growing relationships. May we joyfully explore experiences where roles become unfamiliar and Christlike caring our only concern.

—**Evelyn Minshull**

HOLDING

HANDS

*Hide your loved ones in the shelter of your presence,
safe beneath your hand.*
—Psalm 31:20 TLB

I stood at the busy intersection waiting for the traffic light
to change when I felt Mom's hand reach for mine. My mind
flashed back to the times when I was a little girl reaching
for her hand. I remembered how secure I felt knowing she
would let me skip beside her when the light changed.

I remembered her patience as I grew and developed.
The many times I did silly things and she had to repeat
instructions to me.

The years have passed so quickly and caused the roles to
change. I've raised my own children and crossed the same
street holding their hands. Why can't I see it's my turn to be
patient when she repeats herself? Why can't I refrain from
saying, "You already told me that"? I can see her cringe a
little as she says, "I don't remember. I'm sorry."

How many times did she repeatedly show me how to do
something—to cook, sew, knit, garden, set the table, make
a bed . . . How can I count all that she has taught me?

Now I'm back to where it all started. Crossing the same street with the one who began it all—Mother. Her step isn't as quick as it used to be, but I ask the Lord to help me not to mind—to help me not forget how she took the time years ago to let me skip along. *And please, Lord,* I pray, *remind me to walk a little slower.*

Lord, give me the patience of a young mother so my mother can take my hand and feel as secure as I did years ago.

—**Mary Herron**

P a c e m a k i n g

Life is a hurried and frenzied race,
One we travel at too fast a pace.
So teach me, Lord, to slow my gait,
To master patience and when to wait.
Help me to learn to improve my ways,
To discipline time and enjoy my days,
To pause for pleasure, to not be wary
And to savor life's ordinary.

—**Martha Van Der Linden**

THE GIFT
OF TIME

"Give me a little time," he said, "and I will tell you the dream and what it means."
—Daniel 2:16 TLB

Mom what can I give you for your birthday? You'll be seventy-five tomorrow. Give me some idea. What do you need?"

"Nothing. There's nothing that I need." She paused. "Just give me a little of your time. That's all I really want."

Give me a little of your time. Her words haunted me. She knew how busy I was with the children and working full-time. How could I accommodate her? Why would Mom request my time, the hardest thing of all for me to give? I had no extra time. I could far easier buy her something at the store.

The next day I handed Mom a beautifully wrapped box.

"What's this?" she asked. "I told you not to buy me anything."

"Come on, Mom, just open it," I coaxed.

"Why there's nothing in here!" she exclaimed as she lifted the lid.

"That's right, Mom." I laughed. "I had trouble wrapping 'time,' so you get an empty box; but it represents my gift of time to you today. We're going to spend the entire day together—you and me. Where do you want to go?"

Her elderly face brightened. "Antiquing."

That day we stopped at every antique shop, flea market, and garage/yard sale within a fifteen-mile radius of home. And what fun we had! We even went to Mom's favorite restaurant for lunch. She told the waitress that I was her daughter and we were spending time together for her seventy-fifth birthday.

Ten hours later, when I dropped Mom off at home, she said, "You couldn't have given me anything I would have enjoyed more than this day with you."

"I enjoyed it too," I said as we hugged and kissed good-bye. And all the way home I couldn't help wonder which one of us had received the greatest gift.

Precious Father, slow me down that I may have time available to spend with my aging parents.

—**Peggy Strain**

A MOTHER-
DAUGHTER CHAT

Yea, I have loved thee with an everlasting love:
therefore with lovingkindness have I drawn thee.
—Jeremiah 31:3 KJV

My growing-up house never seemed warmer than when one of those unrelenting winter rains whipped my back with its icy needles and pushed me, breathless, in through the front door.

"Take off your wet things, sweetie, before you catch cold, and come drink some hot cocoa while you tell me all about your day," my mother would holler from the kitchen over sounds and smells of dinner preparations.

After settling into my designated chair and allowing the hot cocoa's curling vapors to warm my wet face, I would begin a nonstop monologue about my latest "crush," my new best friend, my huge pile of homework, my unfair test grade, and on and on. Mom managed to interject several "mm-hmm's" with voice inflections appropriate for each situation, so that by the time the last drop of cocoa trickled down my throat, I felt warm and fuzzy inside, having talked it out with Mom.

Now, on another rainy winter day some forty years later, I sit in Mom's miniature apartment kitchen in a retirement home comprised of many miniature apartments reproduced on eight floors. Thinned of possessions and shrunken in stature, she seems suitable for her new environment. As we sip hot tea (Mom's system can no longer handle cocoa), she chats about Mrs. So-and-So down the hall, her best friend on the seventh floor, how easily she tires, how "nothing is the same anymore," and on and on. As I reply with appropriate "mm-hmm's," a thickness forms in my throat which in turn glazes my eyes with tears. My heart longs to return to winter days when I did all the chattering and Mom said all the "mm-hmm's."

Since Mom and I are both daughters of the heavenly Father, I envision a future when Mom and I, as peers, will mutually chat and mutually listen, always warm, in our new home in heaven.

Heavenly Father, when our heart draws us longingly to the past, may You draw us to Your present mercies and assure us of a future where Your loving-kindness reigns forever.

—**Kathleen A. Walker**

COMING HOME

FOR THANKSGIVING

Let us come before His presence with thanksgiving.
—Psalm 95:2 NKJV

It was the first Thanksgiving since we moved far away from Dad, who lived alone. It was going to be an untraditional Thanksgiving because we weren't going home. My seminary-student husband, Jim, had a research paper to do.

We were saddened to get a phone call on Thanksgiving Eve that Dad would be spending the holiday alone. My only brother, a soldier at Fort Benning, Georgia, had a forty-eight-hour pass, but he couldn't get a flight. We hung up the phone and exchanged looks and comments of disappointment.

"If we could get a flight out of here and back in the same day, or early the next morning, I could still get this paper done," Jim reasoned.

"But tomorrow is Thanksgiving. Do you think we can still get a flight? And, even if we can, do we have the money?"

"I think so, but it will have to be a big part of our Christmas," Jim said.

We did get a flight, and to our amazement we were packed and off to the airport within a couple of hours. We arrived early in the morning, our hearts bursting with thankfulness for how it all worked out. We were beginning to make preparations for the meal when my brother called urging us to hurry back to the airport. He had spent the night in Atlanta waiting for a standby. He, too, was coming home.

Because of all the traveling, the menu was not the traditional dinner with all the trimmings. No one minded. We were simply grateful to be together. Dad was so pleased. He knew his children had made every effort to be with him.

Whether you have a traditional turkey dinner with all the trimmings or not, Thanksgiving can be experienced. It is an attitude of the heart. It is coming home.

Father, help me to have a thankful heart in all of the untraditional happenings in my life. Help me to make every effort to be in Your presence so I can show Your love to others.

—**Barbara Hibschman**

MOTHER NO
LONGER SINGS SOLOS

"I will be your God through all your lifetime, yes, even when your hair is white with age. I made you and I will care for you. I will carry you along and be your Savior."
—Isaiah 46:4 TLB

When I was a little girl, every Thursday night I went to choir practice with my mother. The director allowed me to sit next to Mother and encouraged me to sing along. I beamed with pride. My mother was the best soloist in the choir! I leaned against her, trying to make my voice sound like hers. No matter how hard I tried, mine squeaked on the high notes she hit so clearly.

Mother held the music and turned the pages. When I got lost, she pointed to the right place. I didn't grasp all the words or understand how to read the notes, but those weekly choir rehearsals nurtured my love for music and for the Lord.

Tonight I picked Mother up at her apartment and took her to choir with me. Her voice is no longer strong. It cracks on the high notes and slides off key. She no longer sings solos.

Mother's hands get tired holding the music. She forgets to turn the pages and loses her place. I ask her if she wants to look on with me. She nods her head yes.

I think about the doctor's prognosis. Mom isn't going to get better, and it's only a matter of time—no one knows how long—before she gets worse. I wonder and worry about what he means by "worse."

Suddenly the words we are singing interrupt my thoughts. I feel God's presence. He reminds me that even though we grow old and weary, He never changes. He never stops loving us. He will be with us always.

I glance at Mother. She may no longer be able to grasp the words. She may not understand how to read the notes she's trying to sing, but I know His Spirit is touching hers. He will allow neither death nor life to separate her from His love.

Thank You, Lord, for the way I know You will carry me and my mother during the days ahead.

—**Marlene Bagnull**

THAT'S OKAY,
I'M NOW EIGHTY!

And let the beauty of the LORD our God be upon us.
—Psalm 90:17 KJV

Becoming an octogenarian has ushered me into a time of discovery. I may stumble, spill my food, or drop something, and it's overlooked. I may poke along like an arthritic turtle, but I get there just the same. All this goes with being eighty.

If I can't catch a word that is said, but hear what I'm not supposed to hear, my ears say, "We're also eighty."

I'm a loser. I make a list, then mislay it. I can't find my glasses when they're where they belong—on my nose. I keep searching for that elusive something that I threw away long ago. My precious possessions play hide-and-seek. They know I'm eighty!

I have too many irons in the fire, so with reluctance I let some of them cool. Now my moments are consumed in doing just the necessities.

My forgetter works overtime. I forget the name of my newest great-grandson while glorying that he perpetuates the family name. As I wait for a friend to stop talking, I forget what I was going to say. And I always forget the punch line of the stories I've told over and over.

Sleep, a teasing elf, plays nasty tricks. I can keep myself awake all night trying to go to sleep, then flop into my recliner during the day and doze off in a second.

Now that I've reached eighty, I am aware that my loved ones consider me fragile, precious, and helpless while I often feel old, achy, and worthless. They are kind and polite, ready to help me when I think I can navigate alone. I submit because I know I must.

By this time, however, I've learned to live comfortably. I can laugh at myself, for laughter is the gasoline in my tank. Meanwhile, I seek to model the biblical Anna, full of years, embracing my Redeemer, the joy of my life.

Heavenly Father, I greet each new day as a gift from You. Please help me mirror Your beauty in spite of my physical and mental limitations.

—Edna Mast

A HELPER

IN THE KITCHEN

Love is patient and kind; . . .
love is not ill-mannered
or selfish or irritable.
—1 Corinthians 13:4–5 TEV

While visiting in our home, Mom announces that she is going to make us a pumpkin pie. "If you'll find me an apron, I can go right ahead while you finish that paperwork," she says.

A few moments later, the interruptions begin. "Help me reach this bowl down," she calls. "The flour canister needs filled." "How do you work your can opener?" "I can't find the cinnamon." "The cap on the milk is too tight for me." "Don't you have a deeper pie pan?" "Could you set the oven thermostat?"

By the time the pie is finally in the oven, I am thoroughly exasperated. It would have been so much simpler to make it myself. I wish Mom wouldn't insist on doing things she's really not able to do. Having my mother help in the kitchen is like coping with a small child—only worse. I have no problem dealing patiently with my youngsters' spills or praising their attempts at cooking, but Mom's ineptitude gets on my nerves.

I count to ten and call on the Lord. Through the Holy Spirit, He helps me look beyond Mom's slowness and clumsiness and see the love behind her efforts. As she has all my life, Mom is still trying to do something nice for me. With this insight, my irritation vanishes, replaced by a renewed appreciation for my mother and a much lighter heart.

Inhaling the spicy pumpkin aroma, my mouth begins to water. By the time the pie is lifted from the oven, I am as pleased as Mom—and twice as hungry.

Dear God, thank You for showing me how to change my attitude. Thank You for Mom, and thank You for Your unchanging love.

—Sara L. Smith

WEDNESDAY WAS

MOTHER'S DAY

See to it that no one misses the grace of God
and that no bitter root grows up
to cause trouble and defile many.
—Hebrews 12:15 NIV

I had intended to go and see Mother last week, but activities cluttered my calendar and there was no time left over. I needed an hour to get there, an hour to drive home, and some quality time to spend with her. Perhaps I could go next week, but now I needed the weekend to be with my family and to recuperate from my busyness.

My sisters and I finally had found a good housekeeper to live with Mother. She kept the house spotless, served healthy meals, and was a companion. So the matter of visiting was just that. Mother and I would go shopping, have lunch out, or invite her friends in.

My two sisters also lived an hour away from Mother. Because of their work schedules, they visited when they could. I was the only one still caring for family full-time so my time was more flexible.

I tried to maintain a once-a-week visiting schedule, but

Some days Dad laments that his house and bridge building days are over. He still wants so much to be useful and needed. Then last Sunday, I heard Dad talking with our six-year-old son.

"Grandpa, does God still make miracles like He did in the olden Bible days?"

Dad sat and mused a while. He pulled Daniel closer and asked him to think about rainbows, flowers bursting from their buds in spring, and mountains so high their peaks are hidden by snow and ringed with clouds.

"And dinosaurs!" Daniel piped up.

"Yes, Daniel," Dad said. "And dinosaurs. There always have been miracles, and there are still miracles today. But you have to look for them or they'll come and go and you'll miss seeing them. And do you know what God's greatest miracle is?"

Daniel solemnly shook his head.

"God's greatest miracle is His Son, Jesus. Because Jesus gave up His life for us, we will have an opportunity to live forever. And His resurrection was the greatest miracle of all."

I smiled, glad my husband and I had been wrong. Dad might not be building two-story houses or concrete bridges anymore, but he's building spiritual bridges to span the generations. He's helping to build our son's character brick by brick. He's driving nails of truth into his mind. And he's plastering with great slabs of the Holy Spirit. Today he's building spiritual bridges to span the generations. And his work, laid upon the sure foundation of Jesus Christ, is better than ever!

Father, help me to build my life on the sure foundation of Jesus Christ.

—**Cathy Jean Gohlke**

U s e   M e ,   L o r d

> Lord,
> Take from my mind
>   the stresses of the past
> So that my life
>   may be fruitful
>   in spite of them.
> But choose from my experience
>   the values that last
> And help me
>   to serve You better
>   because of them.

—**Merna B. Shank**

NEEDING

MORE SUPPORT

Do not cast me away when I am old;
do not forsake me when my
strength is gone.

Psalm 71:9 NIV

$\mathbf{P}$lease, I'd rather do it myself!"

How often I heard my teenagers say this. Rarely did they preface it with "please" as they sought to assert their independence and break free from parental restraints. But sometimes they said the words but didn't mean them. Sometimes, as my daughter who is now in college admits, she wished she could go back to being a little girl.

"It's scary growing up; scary knowing I'm going to graduate and be on my own in just another year and a half."

I'm sure part of her fear is paying off the massive college loans hanging over her head, but that's not all of it. Growing up, and growing old, means change; and change, even when it's something we've looked forward to, can be scary. There are just too many unknown factors, too many doubts and fears that may strangle our joy and excitement and optimism.

As our parents grow older and need more support, we need to be sensitive to what's happening inside them—to the feelings they are wrestling with as they struggle to maintain their independence and yet increasingly are faced with their limitations. The more threatened they feel, the more fiercely they may refuse to let us help them, or to relinquish their freedom—like the freedom to continue driving their car. Even though they may have had a couple of close ones, and even though they may know they are not as capable behind the wheel as they once were, they are likely to deny the truth.

"I'm still a good driver," they're likely to argue. "I can

do it. I can take care of myself. I can manage without your help."

And yet despite their insistence, despite what they sav the child within them may be crying out for help, may be longing for assurance that we will take care of them—that we will not abandon them.

Wise is the family that sits down and talks and prays about the future—that plans ahead and strengthens the trust relationship that will be needed for the days ahead and the decisions that may need to be made. And wise are the caregivers who remember their own growing up years as they seek, with God's help, to care for their parents as they grow old and need more support.

NEW

MEMORIES

Fix your thoughts on what is true and good and right.
Think about things that are pure and lovely, and dwell
on the fine, good things in others. Think about all you
can praise God for and be glad about.
—Philippians 4:8 TLB

I can drive just fine!" Mom yells, storming out of the room. A torrent of accusations lies in her wake—this time, how I tricked the doctor into revoking her driving privileges. I've heard it for the umpteenth time today; it won't be the last. And then there's tomorrow . . .

"I didn't get lost. Dr. Reynolds moved his office!" she snaps, fighting to hold onto her independence.

She's forgotten the U-turn across four lanes of traffic, narrowly missing a broadside hit from a delivery truck. I haven't forgotten; I was there.

She doesn't see the four rusty fenders on her old Volkswagen as rippling reminders of misjudged distances, forgotten looks in the rearview mirror, and just plain inattention. "I'll buy new ones," she rationalizes.

But reasoning with her is impossible. So whenever her

mood takes a nosedive—which can be several times a day—I steer her into comfortable, old memories.

"Mom, speaking of driving, remember our vacation in 1961 when we took the long way to Minnesota and drove clear across Canada?" Soon we're happily driving down a memory; the angry accusations and tearful pleading cease.

But sometimes I'm too tired to take that memory jaunt with her. That's when only one thing works—prayer.

As an adult, I never prayed with my mother. Bedtime prayers as a child and blessings at the dinner table summed up my experience. One day, out of sheer frustration, I sat beside her, grabbed her hand, and put my other arm about her.

"Mom, I know you're upset. Let's ask God to handle the situation, okay? I don't have the answers, but I know He does."

Praying not only stops her downward spiral, it also restores my strength. Best of all it draws us together as we focus on God.

Yes, Mom's memory is declining. Her personality seems to change with each passing week. And now I must parent her. Daily I struggle to find new ways to make our days good ones. Unlike parents who strive to create good memories for their children, I can't make new memories for this mom-child I care for. So I must tap into the good ones from the past.

Most importantly, we make the best of the present by regularly entering into God's presence through prayer, recounting the lovely and praiseworthy things He has done for us.

Ironically, Mom is making new memories for me. We share the joy of praying together, hands interlocked, and heads bowed closely—often shedding cleansing tears as we petition God and thank Him for who He is. I am comforted knowing that these new memories will sustain me long after she is gone.

Father God, thank You for blessings in the midst of pain as I discover enduring treasure in those pure, lovely, excellent things called memories.

—**Kathryn E. Bisbee**

BLESSED

FORGETFULNESS

And we know that all things work together for good.
—Romans 8:28 NKJV

When we were young, Dad seemed invincible. We wanted his love and approval desperately—and seldom felt it.

My oldest brother, Tim, clashed with him. By mutual consent, he moved out when he was sixteen. My second brother, Ted, withdrew into books, letting Dad think him weak.

Dad rejected me when I became a Christian. "I could be a very good father to you," he told me once, "if you would just give up having God as your Father."

Ten years ago, Tim tried to be reconciled to Dad. Dad's rejection was shattering to him.

Five years ago, I confronted Dad about some things he had done to me which hurt me. He denied them. The gulf between us became a universe.

When he was fifty-two, Ted had a novel published. "Maybe now Dad will approve of me," he said.

Then Dad lost his memory. All of it. I asked him what

he remembered of his childhood, and he said ruefully, "What childhood?" Dad couldn't remember what he had just watched on television. He couldn't even remember whether he took cream in his coffee.

For the first time, I am seeing Dad weak. He is acutely aware of his loss. When he can't remember my name or our relationship, he cries. When he reads the plaque on his wall commemorating his eightieth birthday party, which he can't recall, he cries. And when he sees his bookcases full of books containing knowledge he used to have, he cries.

But when Dad lost his memory, he forgot he was angry with me. He forgot he considered Ted's interests unmanly. He forgot his differences with Tim.

Last year, the four of us were together for the first time in thirty-five years. When Tim arrived, Dad walked down the wooden steps of his cabin and wrapped the fifty-six-year-old prodigal in a warm embrace. By the time I reached the two aging, bearded men, Ted had joined them.

"Come get in on this hug!" Dad called to me.

We went inside the cabin together, talking and laughing. Dad even joked about his forgetfulness. "I go around in a happy cloud most of the time," he said.

We had tea. "Is that my cup?" he asked. "I figure the nearest cup is always mine."

Ted teased him gently. "I thought the fullest one was always yours!"

Later Tim asked, "Did you ever think you'd father a dynasty?"

"Did I?" Dad looked around at each of us, his three grown children. "I'm so glad you came. Gee, it's good to have all my family here with me!"

Now his tears were tears of joy. I wept, too, for in erasing Dad's memory, God erased our painful past and gave us a loving and lovable father.

Heavenly Father, thank You for Your ability to bring blessing out of seeming tragedy.

—Jessica Shaver

♲
MAMA DOESN'T
RUN ANYMORE

*Tears of joy shall stream down their faces, and I will
lead them home with great care. They shall walk beside
the quiet streams and not stumble.*
—Jeremiah 31:9 TLB

I pick Mama up at 9:00 A.M. to do her weekly shopping
and errands. Her slow, stumbling steps and stopping to
look at almost everything do not make shopping with her
a pleasure.

I hold Mama's elbow as I walk her to the car. "Watch
out for those rocks by that crack," I warn.

"I see them," she snaps back.

Mama walks with head down, cane steadying her fal-
tering feet. Arthritis stiffens her back and knees so her legs
often move puppet-like.

We are silent in the car. Mama peers out the window. I
sneak a glance at her. There is a faraway look about her.

*Is she thinking of the days when she hopped in her car
and drove wherever and whenever she pleased?* I wonder.

My thoughts skip back through the years to when Mama
raced us teenagers down the street on the way home from

a movie. I remember how she liked to dance. She even took lessons once to learn new steps. And in her seventies, she regularly marched around the small lake near her home.

Pulling into the market's parking lot, my mother tosses her handicap permit on the car dash—another reminder of her frailties. I hurry to help her out and get a shopping cart for her to lean on. Then I wander the store aisles while Mama shops. I fear my impatience will show. Several times she apologizes for being so slow, but that doesn't stop her from reading another label of an item I know she has no intention of purchasing.

All at once, I feel God nudging me. He reminds me to be glad Mama is still interested in many things; to rejoice she is still able to walk. I know He patiently watches over her stumbling steps. He always has time for her.

As I join my mother at the checkout, tenderness wells up inside me. As we walk together to the car, I have a fleeting picture of Mama one day running down a street in heaven.

Heavenly Father, thank You for Your patience with our stumbling steps and for Your love.

—June L. Varnum

ONLY A
POLE LAMP?

*"And I will pray the Father,
and He will give you another Helper,
that He may abide with you forever."*
—John 14:16 NKJV

Mom is sitting at the kitchen table eating the homemade turkey noodle soup I brought for her, but she isn't really with me. She keeps looking out the window and saying, "He's watching me again."

How should I answer? I've already told her over and over again the past few months that it's not a man standing in her neighbor's window but a pole lamp. She won't believe me. Obviously, she wants to think someone is watching her.

A lady comes in to check on Mom three times a day. My sister lives next door, but she works during the day. My brother and I come when we can. Still there are many hours when Mom is alone. I know she's lonely.

I want her to go into a personal care home where there will be company for her. My brother and sister do not. I feel frustrated. I have prayed many times for an end to her loneliness. I'm beginning to dread these visits when I hear about the man who watches her.

But wait a minute! She's really a child again. She needs to have someone to watch over her constantly. Since she doesn't have someone, she made him up. He's right next door in case she needs him.

When I stop being upset and frustrated for a moment, I know that she really does have Someone. And she doesn't have to make Him up. Jesus is always with her. I hope it doesn't offend Him to know that sometimes He looks a lot like a pole lamp!

Lord, in my heart I know You're with her. Help me to be at peace and stop worrying about her. I'm human. I cannot be in two places at once, but You can, Lord, and I know You will be.

—Mary Marvin

THE TIE

THAT BINDS

*The love of God has been poured out in our hearts by
the Holy Spirit who was given to us.*
—Romans 5:5 NKJV

For nearly forty years Mother and I corresponded once or twice weekly. As a result, a deep bond of friendship grew.

Life had taken me miles away from our home area. Visits were limited. Phone calls were prohibitive as there was much to share.

Through her letters to me, Mom became not only a best friend but also a cherished mentor. She would often include a timely clipping that spoke to a perceived need or shared interest. Words of advice, encouragement, challenge, and humor made each letter a highlight of my busy week.

Conversely, through my letters, I was able to draw her into the activities of my busy family. She grew to feel a part of the ministry I was privileged to share as the wife of a pastor.

A few years ago I began to notice signs of fatigue in her

writing. Thoughts and words no longer flowed freely. Concentration was eluding her as her tired mind struggled for expression. Now Mother no longer writes letters. Scraps of stationery found in her room indicate she has tried but failed in an attempt to share her heart. The closure of this exchange has left me with a deep void.

I feel constrained to continue writing to her although there is no response. Now I write short notes on bright cards. I need to let her know that she is always in my thoughts and prayers. I need to remind her how much I treasure all that we have shared—how much my life has been enriched because she has been my mother. Most of all, I want to remind her that she can never drift beyond God's loving care.

I know that one day, perhaps soon, the earthly door will be shut. Until then, with each note goes a prayer that the Spirit of God will quicken to her heart what my words may fail to convey.

Thank You, Father, that Your love poured out in our hearts is the tie that binds us.

—Rosemary Browne

MOTHER AND
MANICOTTI

Be patient in trouble, and prayerful always.
When God's children are in need,
you be the one to help them out.
—Romans 12:12–13 TLB

Manicotti? I never heard of it, Mother."

"Neither did I, until I saw this," she replied, showing me a tempting magazine ad. "It looks delicious. Would you make some for me?"

I had come to houseclean Mother's trailer, hoping to finish that same day. Ravaged by cancer, she no longer could clean or cook for herself. Nevertheless, she stubbornly refused to leave the home she had affectionately named "Tin Can" to live with me. Privacy was one of the last assets Mother managed to retain, and she was determined not to lose it. So I helped her as much as she would allow.

But I don't have time to make manicotti today, I complained silently as Mother babbled on. *I don't even know how to cook it. I'll have to run to the market for hamburger, and where on earth do I find manicotti? But if it will tempt her appetite, I'll have to try.*

To my surprise, in the market I easily found manicotti stacked with the other types of macaroni.

Later, in Mother's pocket-sized kitchen, I boiled the tube-shaped manicotti while she watched intently. "Not too long," she protested. "The recipe says just until limp."

Rolling my eyes heavenward, I groaned inwardly, *Mother, I can read.* Even so, I patiently stuffed each manicotti with a spicy hamburger mixture, poured a can of tomato sauce over the lot, then put them in the oven to bake.

"They look just like the picture," Mother declared as we sat at her tiny kitchen table. "Aren't they good? I'm so glad you made them. There's even enough for my dinner tomorrow."

The manicotti were good. Even better was my pleasure in knowing I had provided something Mother enjoyed eating. I could almost imagine God smiling down on us, blessing our sweet fellowship together.

Thank You, Lord, for a mother who cherished me and taught me love and compassion.

—**Georgia E. Burkett**

THANK
YOU

Nothing in all creation is hidden from God's sight.
—Hebrews 4:13 NIV

Mom lived in a small cottage on our forty-acre farm. "Can't she ever say thank you?" I fumed. My cheeks burned, as I hurried away from her withering glare from behind ruffled curtains. The sun hid its face and a frigid wind cut across my bare hands as I marched along the well-worn path home.

I sat at the kitchen table. Round and round, I turned a warm coffee cup. The ever-present gloom that had moved in with my dependent mother threatened to pounce upon me and swallow me whole.

The door burst open and a trail of cold air followed my husband inside. I shivered.

"How's Ma?" he asked, knowing full well what my answer would be.

"Ma is just being Ma," I said briskly. I fought to hold my tongue. *It must be tiring; the same old story over and over*, I thought. But my heart ached, and I had to tell someone.

"She refuses to notice anything I do for her," I complained. "I think she must lay awake every night fantasizing faults she is waiting to find in me."

His eyes twinkled with understanding. "No wonder she can't sleep." He chuckled.

I smiled back at him and got on with my work. Yet no matter how I tried, I couldn't put off the heavy shroud of anger and self-pity that pulled at my shoulders and tripped me up at every turn. *Why is it,* I wondered, *the ones who do the most seem to be appreciated the least?*

One hour later, as I headed out the door with a peace offering, I brushed up against the refrigerator and knocked off a note.

Dear Shirley,

   I have examined your heart and know everything about you. I know when you sit or stand. When you are far away, I know your every thought. I chart the path ahead of you and tell you where to stop and rest. Every moment, I know where you are. I know what you are going to say before you even say it. I precede you and follow you, and place My hand of blessing on your head. Thank you for your faithfulness.

                                                              Jesus

Looking up, I saw my husband quickly bury his face in the newspaper.

Since that day, I've dropped the shroud and clothed myself in those wondrous words personalized from Psalm 139:1–5. And on those days when Mom is the most unloving, I stop and listen. Deep within that still, small voice whispers, "Thank you."

Teach me today, Father, to turn my eyes away from people and onto You.

—**Shirley Folwarski**

R e a l i t y

There are those who see
    only roses in life,
        pretending the thorns aren't there;
and those who see
    no roses at all . . .
    constantly cursing the thorns.
Then there is the Christian
    who sees both,
    knowing whom to praise
        for the blossoms—
    and where to run
    when the thorns cause us pain.

—**Marcia Krugh Leaser**

SURVIVING

MISS DAISY

"Honor your father and your mother."
—Exodus 20:12 NKJV

I love my mother and am committed to honoring her. Because she kept me in Sunday school, against the strong opposition of my father, I came to know the Lord Jesus in my preteen years. But as an adult, I found myself becoming depressed whenever I stayed with Mother more than a few days. Like Miss Daisy of the movie, she controlled her house—and tried to control me!

Mom forbade me to wash a dish or sweep a floor. I obeyed but was frustrated. It was she who had taught me not to be lazy as well as to be obedient. I also felt resentful. It was as if Mom didn't trust my ability to do anything. An excellent cook and housekeeper, she taught these skills to my older sister. Sis and her family always had lived close by Mom. I had gone away to college, then married, and lived far away.

Now I was supposed to settle Mom back in her home after her cancer treatment. For five weeks I would clean and cook and wait on her. How would I handle her demands, her attempts to control me? Would I become depressed?

I began to understand that "honor your father and your mother" applied to me as an adult, but "children, obey your parents" (Eph. 6:1 NKJV) no longer did. Since Mom is a Christian, I decided to treat her as my sister-in-Christ. I pointed out that her demanding tone of voice made me feel angry and resentful. Eventually she began saying please and thank you.

I didn't always immediately do what Mom wanted me to do. "I'll bring your book when I'm through with what I'm doing," I would say.

Mom learned to preface her requests with, "When you're finished with what you are doing, will you please . . ."

When Mom insisted my older sister come and do things for her, I refused to give in to feelings of inferiority.

"We're giving Sis a break. That's why I'm here," I would tell her firmly.

Once Mom saw that I wasn't going to allow my sister to be always running over to do this or that, she accepted me doing more for her.

At times both Mom and I became angry, but we talked it out. I refused to allow Mom to treat me as a small child and asked the Lord to help me not act like one!

I left Mom living independently in her home. That was a victory. And just as great a victory, I left not feeling depressed. I felt better about our adult relationship than I ever had. As sisters-in-Christ, Mom and I had learned together as we had lived together.

Lord, help us to honor our parents as You have commanded us. Deliver us from the false guilt that Satan likes to heap on us when being with them gets tough!

—Aretta Loving

S m i l e s

As light makes bright a gloomy day,
　As warmth dispels the chill,
As color cheers a room that's gray,
　As healing lifts the ill—
Just so a smile shines bright with gladness
　And warms us through with cheer.
It helps to drive out fear and sadness
　With thoughts that God is near.

—Merna B. Shank

TRUST IN

THE LORD

Trust in the LORD.
Have faith, do not despair.
—Psalm 27:14 TEV

As I enter his room, he's wild-eyed. "Are you going to the party?" he mutters.

"I don't think I'm invited," I reply, touching his hand lightly.

"Sure you are. They're having a party at the barber shop. Bologna, cheese, and everything." He closes his eyes and begins pulling his legs purposefully to free them from their restraints.

It's my shift to sit with Pop tonight, and I'm not looking forward to it. How will I get through this? I'm working full-time—overtime no less, making our daughter's wedding gown, cooking for my mother-in-law, and now caring for Pop as he recovers from double knee replacement and withdrawal from addiction to pain medication. There are too many demands being made on my time.

Suddenly he's awake again. "You're the worst

daughter-in-law in the world," he yells as he shakes his fist at me.

I gently unfold the beautiful white satin train and open a box of iridescent sequins. The overhead light makes them sparkle. As I stitch, I concentrate on happier days—my husband's recollections of his dad cheering him on at baseball games, fishing trips to Michigan, Pop picking apples each July with our daughters . . .

Each sequin a memory—each hour a step toward the end of Pop's ordeal. I cling to that hope. *We'll do it,* I resolve. *We'll get Pop walking. We'll get this gown finished. And we'll have a party. We'll just move it to the reception hall and change the menu a little!*

Pop is trusting us, perhaps not consciously. But at times he knows we're here, caring for him, praying for him. And we're trusting God for the strength and energy we need as we look forward to happier days.

Father, I thank You for family, even when being part of a big family seems to overwhelm me with responsibility. Still the blessings far outweigh the negative load. Thank You for encouraging me to trust in You.

—**Judy Eble Kiel**

NEVER

WITHOUT HOPE

"I will never leave you nor forsake you."
—Hebrews 13:5 NKJV

All the way home from the hospital, Dad sat grim-faced and silent. He was still trying to adjust to the loss of his left leg by amputation just two weeks before.

"Stop the car," he said when we arrived at the end of the driveway. Reaching into the back seat, he grabbed his walker and hobbled to his own automobile parked in the garage. He eased into the driver's seat, backed the car out of the garage, and drove it up and down the length of the driveway several times. Exhausted, but smiling, he emerged from his car. He was still able to drive! That meant he would continue to have some control over his life.

"Better leave the car out," he said lightheartedly, hitting the button to close the garage. "I might need it tomorrow."

My heart spilled over with gratitude to our heavenly Father. "Thank You, Lord," I whispered. "Thank You for not deserting him."

The amputation was only the latest in a series of setbacks Dad experienced as a result of his illness. But at each new level of debilitation, the Lord never failed to provide him with some cause for hope and a small measure of independence. Though he was continually adjusting his expectations downward, my father was always able to discover something he could still do for himself. At each new discovery, we thanked God for His faithfulness.

How blessed we are that we have a God who gives us just what we need. Whether we personally are suffering from illness or despair, or watching our loved ones suffer, each of us can count on the Lord's promise not to forsake us nor leave us without comfort. And we know that at our homecoming, Christ will take us to Himself and make us all whole again.

Lord God, we thank You for Your love and compassion and for Your daily assurance that You will never leave us without hope.

—June Eaton

I WILL

COMFORT YOU

As a mother comforts her child,
so will I comfort you.
—Isaiah 66:13 NIV

My mother can no longer comfort me. And yet, I still need her. I need a loving hand to stroke back stray hairs. I need the small gesture of fixing my collar. I especially need a sympathetic ear and a cup of special spiced tea.

But now she needs me instead. She misplaces her glasses, forgets to pay the electric bill, or gets upset that someone has stolen her comb. I stroke back the thinning gray hairs. I take over buttoning her sweater when gnarled hands fail. I listen to her stories even though I know them by heart.

I honestly try to respect her "advice" and not see it as interference, remembering that with age comes wisdom. But I get frustrated with her increasing senility.

I am thankful for her, even though she is not the strong, independent woman she once was. The woman I still need. The woman she still wants to be. It's hard for her too. Sometimes I forget that.

Now I am the comforter. But sometimes I need to remember who is the mother . . . who is the child.

Oh, greatest Comforter, help me to be as patient and understanding with Mom as You are with me. And please help me, every once in awhile, to see my mother as I sometimes see You, through a child's eyes.

—**Faye Roberts**

In the Garden

Hibiscus trumpets blossom,
red crepe petals last one day.
Closing at night,
they fall to earth—
we find tight packets
in the morning sun.
We learn late
to be present
in the present.
Like the ruby-throated hummingbird,
we hover over open mouths,
wings blurring
as we fly backward
to parent our parents.

—**Shirley S. Stevens**

❧

SUNDAY

MORNING GUILT

"For where two or three are gathered together in My name, I am there in the midst of them."
—Matthew 18:20 NKJV

*G*uilty if I do, and guilty if I don't, I thought as I drove the thirty miles to my mother's house. There was no way I could get Mom's breakfast, comb her long braided hair, take care of the cat and the litter box, stay and visit a bit, and still get back in time to go to church.

Why had they decided to have services at 9:00 A.M. during the summer? I asked myself. But I knew the answer. Most people wanted to go earlier to have the rest of the day to enjoy the sunshine.

So here I was, making my early morning visit to my mother and feeling guilty for not going to church. If I went to church, then I'd feel guilty for leaving Mom alone.

I turned on the car radio hoping to find a church service. I didn't, but I did find a religious music program. Suddenly the car was flooded with a beautiful voice singing, "What a Friend We Have in Jesus."

As I entered my mother's house, I was singing. Mom

smiled and joined in. I took her hand. There in her kitchen we stood singing, "What a friend we have in Jesus, all our sins and griefs to bear!"*

"I like the old hymns," Mom said.

"Me too," I said.

Then I remembered Jesus saying wherever two or three gathered in His name, He would be with them. Suddenly my guilty heart felt at peace. He was here! I knew it. If I couldn't go to church, Jesus knew why and He understood.

We had "church" at Mom's house for the rest of the summer, and He came every Sunday.

God, thank You that we do have a friend in Jesus, and He will give us peace if we just slow down long enough to let Him.

—**Mary Marvin**

* "What a Friend We Have in Jesus," Joseph Scriver, 1820 –1886.

MY

PRICELESS DAD

"Therefore I say to you, do not worry about your life,
what you will eat or what you will drink; nor about
your body, what you will put on. Is not life more than
food and the body more than clothing?"
—Matthew 6:25 NKJV

I want to show you something," Mom said in a low voice, pulling me into her bedroom. I sat on the edge of the bed as she pulled open one of Dad's dresser drawers. "Look at this!" she giggled. "Your dad keeps his dirty clothes in this drawer."

I leaned forward for a better view. The odor of soiled underwear was unmistakable. I laughed too. "Why does he do that?"

Mom rolled her eyes, shrugged her shoulders, and sighed, as if to say, "Why does your father do anything?"

Today I sat on the edge of that same bed. Mom has been gone a year and a half. Dad isn't able to live alone without my assistance, but I encourage him to do what he can. Although he washes his own clothes, he seldom puts them in the same place twice. If I don't set out clean clothes each day, he has no problem with wearing dirty ones.

"Dad, what have you done with your clothes?" I call to the other end of the house. I feel frustrated. Over the past few days some of his clothes have vanished. I've searched in closets, hampers, everywhere—including the trash can. I don't have a clue.

I pull open the "dirty clothes" drawer and find some of his missing clothes. Some are clean. Some are dirty. I look up to discover Dad watching me, his little dog in his arms. He grins at me.

"Dad, you can't keep your clean and dirty clothes in the same drawer," I scold. "Where did you put your clothes this time?"

"I don't know," he says, obviously puzzled.

"But, Dad, you have to know," I almost shout. "You're the only one who lives here."

Dad is getting angry with me, but I tell myself I have a right to be upset. After all, I'm doing my best to care for him. He can help a little bit. Can't he?

We lock the front door and head to my house for supper. As always, Dad seems to be tagging behind me like a little kid. I mourn my loss of privacy and independence. Then I remember when it was the other way around. I followed Dad like his shadow, but he never complained. I know he needs me now like I needed him then—and still need him.

Suddenly the clothes aren't important. I can always buy more clothes, but I can't buy another Dad.

Father, thank You for the time we share together on this earth. Help me to savor each moment.

—Josie Halbert

Just Asking

What is time
  but something
    to worry about?
What is pain
  but something
    to bear?
What is love
  but the equalizer
    of both?

—Marcia Krugh Leaser

≈

THE PILLAR
FALLS

Let my cry come before You, O LORD;
Give me understanding according to Your word.
—Psalm 119:169 NKJV

Dad sat in the chair with dampened hair and a towel over his shoulders. His right hand clutched his thigh directly above his knee. "I'm trying not to shake!" he said as he gripped tighter.

I made an anxious attempt to trim and shape his hair which would no longer lay flat. The dignity of entering a barber shop for a proper executive haircut was no longer an option. Dad needed to rest twenty minutes for every four minutes of trim.

"You know this should prove one thing to you," he said.

"What's that?" I asked.

"Never grow old!"

"I'm afraid it's too late. It started the day I was born."

"Well, stop it!"

Three hours later a simple haircut was complete. The man who was central to my teenage rebellion twenty years ago no longer knew his purpose. My genetic independence and busy schedule could no longer deny or refuse him the intimacy his professional position stole for so many years.

There was always another machine to repair and highway to know the hum of his Oldsmobile. Weekends with the family became more and more infrequent. A six-foot, two-inch, two-hundred-fifty-pound stranger would enter the door with a vaguely familiar smile. He was the king of his castle for two days, unless the office called.

The large hand that once drove me further away now reached out just to have me near.

"I must go, Dad."

"Why?" he asked in a childlike tone.

Was this what he really wanted to ask for decades? Did he fight to hold what he could not bear to lose, but time slipped through his fingers?

Yesterday cannot be recovered. The fight is gone! The office replaced over thirty years experience with artificial intelligence. Only real words and feelings are left. There is no more armor to hide behind; no more humming Oldsmobiles.

"Do you need anything downstairs?"

"An orange Popsicle would be wonderful."

Once his little girl, I'm now gray-haired. My hand, though small next to his, has grown too much to slip through, and it steadies this new man of humility. Both of us realize time is short.

Heavenly Father, thank You for our vulnerability and the opportunity to overcome the past. You create in us a new day of compassion. You give the strength to accept our need for grace to give that compassion away.

—**Ellen Lethbridge**

A Perfect Picture

Life's like a puzzle
We can't understand;
The pieces don't fit
When they're placed by our hand.

But when God takes the pieces
And puts them in place,
They fit smoothly together
Because of His grace.

For He knows how He made us
And what we're to do,
Plus the timing is perfect
From His point of view.

—**Frances Gregory Pasch**

HEALING

PAINFUL MEMORIES

"Do to others as you would have them do to you."
—Luke 6:31 NIV

For many years I lived in turmoil. I chose a stress-filled profession, nursing. I married a foreign-born man and raised three children. I never made the connection between my turmoil and my deprived and violent childhood. Three years ago I found some welcome truth and light when I began attending Adult Children of an Alcoholic Parent meetings—an offshoot of Alcoholics Anonymous.

I allowed painful memories to rise in me and told others about them. I remembered my drunken father and his abusive slaps and ugly words. I remembered him angrily slamming a car door on my leg when I was eight. I remembered the smell of alcohol. I remembered coming to the rescue of my younger sister when he was choking her and wouldn't let go. I remembered coming between him and my mother as he slapped her around the room. I remembered standing up to him, saying, "Don't you hit my mother!"

Decades later, those unhealed memories contributed to

my marriage breakup. Chaos and broken relationships and addictions added to my burdens. But thanks to Jesus Christ and devoted friends, God's grace and power have been my anchor through difficult times.

Now both my parents are old. Daddy is eighty and Mom is seventy-five. I work in a nursing home and understand the needs of elderly persons. Every day I am challenged with the Golden Rule.

I have been able to talk with my mother about childhood abuse, but not my father. Not yet. The son of one of the residents in the nursing home told me about his healing from a parent's abuse. He told me how he forgave his mother and how, in her old age, she was even fun to be with. God really spoke to me through him.

Now, as I do my parents' laundry, drive them to doctors' appointments, and talk with them, I find the will to walk the golden pathway in Jesus' presence and strength.

O Lord, my God, You are the Great Physician. Thank You for the hope and power I always find in You. Thank You for Your ongoing, perfect healing.

—**Grace Han**

GREATER
LOVE

"Greater love has no one than this,
than to lay down one's life for his friends."
—John 15:13 NKJV

Mom and Dad wanted to stay in their own home. I dropped in to help as often as possible. I cooked and cleaned and did any other project that would help them maintain health and independence.

One morning several years ago I was bustling around their kitchen, washing dishes and cleaning the refrigerator. While I scrubbed the boil-overs that had burned on the kitchen range, I heard Mom's thin voice from her hospital bed in the living room. "You're always so busy when you come. Why don't you let that wait and just come and sit down and visit for awhile?"

A maze of thoughts stumbled over each other in my mind. Yes, I was busy. My time was limited. But I also remembered Jesus' words in the above Scripture. I'd often thought that life is made up of time. That when I invest a minute or an hour in someone's life, I really am giving up my life for them. I am living the "greater love" about which Jesus spoke.

I mopped the brown goop off the range and sat down beside Mom. For the half hour before I had to leave we talked and laughed and told stories. As I got up to leave, Mom focused her almost unseeing eyes on me. She smiled. "Thanks for just visiting. I really appreciate all you do around here, but sometimes I just get so lonely."

Myriad tasks still needed doing each time I stopped, but I tried to set aside some moments to visit. Sometimes I mended while we talked. Or folded clothes. Or rubbed her neck or back. And sometimes we just talked. We both treasured those visits. I treasure them even more now. Three months ago, while dishes waited in the sink and the floor needed swept, I sat down beside Mom. She was more ill than usual. It was hard for her to speak clearly. I combed her hair and read her a couple of her favorite psalms. I'd rubbed her feet only a few minutes when her hunched shoulders suddenly relaxed more than I had seen in years. I felt for her pulse. She had none.

I, too, am at peace.

Dear God, give me wisdom to balance the have-to-do's with precious moments I'll treasure forever.

—Helen Heavirland

∂

DEEP PURPLE

PETUNIAS

*"Look at the field lilies! . . . King Solomon in all his
glory was not clothed as beautifully as they. And if God
cares so wonderfully for flowers that are here today
and gone tomorrow, won't he more surely care for
you?"*
—Matthew 6:28 –30 TLB

What happened, Mother?" I asked one bright, sunny
morning when I stopped in to visit her. "You're crying!"

"What am I going to do about my garden?" she said,
wiping her eyes. "It's springtime, and I just don't have the
strength to get out there and dig."

No wonder she was crying. Mother always had loved
puttering about her garden, producing some of the loveliest
flowers in the neighborhood. But now, weakened by terminal illness, she thought her gardening days were over.

I remembered how that very morning I had asked the
Lord to show me how I could entertain Mother that day.
Here was my answer already. "Dry those tears, Mother," I
said. "You're going to have as pretty a garden this summer
as ever. Do you feel well enough to go with me to the
garden center? You can pick out the flowers you want, then

after lunch you can tell me where to plant them. This will be my Mother's Day gift to you."

I'm not sure which of us enjoyed that beautiful spring day more. Studiously, as though purchasing jewels, she selected settings of her favorite petunias, zinnias, marigolds, scarlet sage, pansies, and others.

After a quick sandwich, we spent the rest of the day in her garden. Watching carefully, she told me exactly where she wanted each plant placed. "Save those deep purple petunias to plant here by the sidewalk," she advised. "They're my favorites. Those pansies too. They'll grow nicely together."

Of course, I kept after the weeds and watering during the frightfully hot summer that followed, but God added His own magical touch. I never saw flowers more beautiful or luxuriant.

Mother's garden that year was the last she had here on earth. By October she began sinking, and shortly before Christmas she moved on to be with the Lord. But the memory of Mother sitting by her purple petunias, reading her Bible, will always remain with me. And I'm positive she is now enjoying the beauty of God's own glorious garden in heaven. I'm sure He has one. Didn't He provide a sample of it here on earth for us to enjoy?

Lord, You know each of us, Your children, by name and You love us dearly. May I comfort those who grieve by helping them find joy in Your love.

—**Georgia E. Burkett**

Let Me Show You Christ

When you are sick and feeling low,
I'll stand by you.
When you lose joy and force a smile,
I'll laugh for you.
When you ache and share your sorrow,
I'll listen to you.
When you cry and cannot cope,
I'll comfort you.
When you are stressed and overwhelmed,
I'll hug you.
When you stare and do not talk,
I'll hold you.
When your darkness seems black as night,
I'll pray with you.
And when your joy returns with praise,
I'll sing with you.

—**Carol Wedeven**

MOTHER,

HOW COULD YOU?

And whatever you do in word or deed,
do all in the name of the Lord Jesus,
giving thanks to God the Father through Him.
— Colossians 3:17 NKJV

Tears stung my cheeks as I hung up the phone. "Mother, how could you accuse me of stealing your cake pan?"

I grabbed at prayers like a starved person asking God for all of the Galatians fruit to bear me up. And then I begged Him to give me all of the whatsoevers in Philippians 4:8.

"Who is this woman, Lord?" I groaned. "I don't know my mother anymore. She has changed so much. I don't even know how to talk to this stranger. Lord, please, I want my mother back."

I had not been a sassy teenager; however, at age forty-five I was feeling like one in my heart. Oh, if we could paddle a parent. But forget that. It would only stir up wrath and perhaps create a medical problem!

The shock of my mother's accusation began to wear off as I stirred around in prayer and in confession. Forgiving peace came, but not as fast as I would have liked it. But then, I couldn't let go of the hurt as fast as I wanted to either.

Now, when I get into similar situations, I'm learning to say, "Come on, Mother. You can go through my cabinets and have any cake pan you'd like."

I still don't have all the answers. Besides, Mom is always full of new surprises and challenges. Sometimes I gape and gawk, uneducated and inexperienced in this area of parenting parents. But I think surely there must have been times when she gaped and gawked at me.

Lord, teach me to laugh and not to take to heart the things Mother says and does.

—Lois Reese

The Power of Words

Sometimes we speak them hastily
  and regret it.
Other times we remain silent
  and wish we had spoken.
Words come in all sizes . . .
  many are small, yet dynamic.
Others are big,
  but of little importance.
We can change lives by what we say . . .
  either for good or for bad.
Our words can make people laugh
  or make them cry.
Words can build them up
  or bring them down . . .
Pull them closer
  or turn them away.
Words can draw pictures . . .
  pretty ones or ugly ones.
They can cut like a knife
  or soothe like a salve.
Whether written or spoken, rehearsed or
  spontaneous, words are powerful.
They are easy to come by,
  but not easily forgotten.
A good reason to measure them out carefully.

—**Frances Gregory Pasch**

THOSE

LITTLE BOYS

"For My thoughts are not your thoughts,
Nor are your ways My ways,"
says the LORD.
—Isaiah 55:8 NKJV

What am I supposed to do with those little boys? They won't get out of bed. They won't come and eat. They won't listen to anything I say."

"That's because they really aren't there, Mother," I tried to assure her every time I visited. I'd take her from room to room trying to prove to her that no one was hiding in the closet, or under the bed, or behind the sofa.

"What do you know?" she'd snap. "I know what I'm talking about. I'm not blind or stupid. Last night they got into my dresser drawers again. You should see the mess they made. And they took my bar of soap and my comb. Why do they do such things? Didn't their mother teach them any better?"

Every day my mother sees people who aren't there and hears voices that aren't speaking. As I listen to her rave, I find myself questioning and even doubting the Lord. Why is He allowing her to suffer? Why doesn't He give her back her mind?

But slowly I'm beginning to see God's goodness and mercy even in this. Because Mom's mind is failing, she doesn't realize she is getting worse. She doesn't always remember who I am, but she also doesn't remember people who have hurt her in the past. And even though she gets irritated with those little boys, because of them she doesn't feel alone.

It isn't easy and I don't always succeed, but I try to accept those little boys. I try to listen to Mom talk about them and not argue with her. And I find that when I choose to see those little boys from God's perspective, they really are a blessing.

Lord, keep reminding me that Your ways are not my ways and help me to know Your peace.

—**Marlene Bagnull**

LIVE-IN
PARENTS

When I pray, you answer me,
and encourage me
by giving me the strength I need.

Psalm 138:3 TLB

I don't like having Grandma live with us," my teenage daughter complained as we were rushing to get out the door. As usual, Grandma was making us late. My husband shot our daughter a you-had-better-shut-your-mouth look. I didn't say anything as the knot in my stomach tightened.

Mom had been living with us for about a year but it seemed like much longer. Some days I couldn't help wonder if we had made the right decision. The idyllic picture I had painted of us living together as one big happy family was as far from reality as Mother's ability to dress herself. And yet, we believed this was where she belonged—at least for now.

How can you find God's strength to care for a live-in parent who demands more than you feel able to give?

Don't put guilt trips on yourself or others. Living with someone who is losing his ability to do the simplest tasks is not easy. It's natural, especially for children and teens, to resent the ways the older person's presence disrupts family life. Don't deny your feelings or give yourself or others a you-shouldn't-feel-that-way lecture. Instead, encourage one another to rely on the strength the Lord will provide.

Get needed rest. It takes a lot of energy and patience to care for an aging parent. I found I was much better able to cope with what Mom said and did—with the dirty dishes she put in my cabinets, the clothes she stuffed in the china closet, and her insistence that a little boy was in her bed—when I'd gotten enough sleep at night. That was especially difficult in the beginning. Just as when my children were newborns, I heard every move she made. I felt compelled to go and check on her. But gradually I learned to tune out most of her nighttime noises (after first parent-proofing the downstairs) and to trust I'd hear her when she really needed me.

Make time for yourself and your family. I admit this wasn't easy to do. Yet even Jesus periodically withdrew from the demands of His ministry. I tried to make it a priority to get away both by myself and with my family. Sometimes just feeding Mom an early dinner so we could eat by ourselves was all it took to restore our sense of family and renew our perspective. Other times we needed a longer time away. The work of finding a caregiver was worth the effort.

Don't be afraid to let others know you need help. The I-don't-need-any-help mentality is self-defeating. Investigate the services of local day care and respite centers. Let your friends and church family know specific ways they can help. Even when you feel like no one is listening or cares, keep asking and trust that in God's perfect timing you will receive exactly the help He knows you need.

Talk to and get support from other caregivers. Join a local support group. If one is not available, ask the Lord to help you form one. The strength that comes from knowing you're not alone can often be a key factor in keeping on.

Keep looking for those hidden blessings. If Mom hadn't lived with us, I would have missed those precious moments of tucking her in bed at night. I would have missed dressing her in frilly blouses and bringing her a bowl of her favorite ice cream. Most of all, I would have missed the opportunity God gave me to take care of her as she once took care of me.

Live-in parents are likely to be more demanding than infants, more exhausting than toddlers, and more unpredictable and moody than teens. There will be days when you question the wisdom of your decision—days when you feel drained physically, emotionally, and spiritually. But God is faithful. He will enable you to keep on for as long as having your parent live-in is the best alternative for him and for you.

WALKING THE

BELOVED HILLS

I will lift up my eyes to the hills—
From whence comes my help?
My help comes from the LORD.
—Psalm 121:1–2 NKJV

Some forty years ago, Mom and Dad built their home into the side of the hill that sloped to a meandering stream centering three acres. Widow and widower, they met and married in middle age. This lush wooded land was a continuing honeymoon site. They transformed it into a natural park with skill born of experience and loving care.

Dad died at ninety-two in his own bed looking out at his hills with his "bride" beside him. Mom found much comfort knowing God had supplied strength and grace to give Dad this last gift of being able to end this life in the place they both so loved.

For five years Mom managed on her own. She attended the acreage, diligently keeping birds and blooms a happy part of that beautiful spot. My husband and I were proud of her; but we knew, as she entered her ninetieth year, it was time to leave the fort and come live with us. Knowing the role the outdoors had played in her life for four decades, I sensed some of the loss she felt as she surveyed her dear hills those last months before the move.

"Walked my beloved hills this morning," read her letters so often. And then one day, "Wanted to get out on my beloved hills today, but it was slippery. Didn't seem wise . . ."

Those hills spoke to her of God's peace and love when life was full and when it was laced with sadness and loneliness. If I could have packed up her hills with her furniture, I would have done it. Then, quite simply, one day I found a wonderful thought hanging in my mind, like a memo on a peg from the loving heavenly Father.

Mom came when summer was fading, still in time to walk the restored nature trail I cut through the woods that surround the cul-de-sac of our condominium. It took nine hours to trim, and my husband generously claims that if you take the tour slowly, you can cover it in almost five minutes!

Here Mom and I planted from her hills a dainty little Austrian pine, a bath of lily-of-the-valley, ginger plant, wild violet, and jack-in-the-pulpit. We walk these hills, kick through fallen leaves, look up into waving branches above, sit on the stumps in the little ravine, and smile at one another . . . remembering. When we return, Mother often sits at her organ and I hear again the precious strains: "I walked today where Jesus walked . . . my heart felt unafraid. . . ."*

Thank You, Father God, that You never leave us or

102

forsake us and that Your Word and Your creation constantly remind us of Your loving faithfulness.

—Nan McKenzie Kosowan

*"I Walked Today Where Jesus Walked," © 1937, Jeoffrey O'Hara.

Fur Angel

Black nose like grease paint:
"Clown," calico cat,
leaps on my father's knees
when he rasps a sigh.
Soft paws massage his chest,
knead out a smile,
bat at his glasses,
fence with his knobby finger.
Laughing, he smooths
brown "wings" on white back.
Clown, my calico cat,
ministers to both of us.

—Leah Thorne

READY

OR NOT

Trust in the LORD with all thine heart; and lean not unto thine own understanding. In all thy ways acknowledge him, and he shall direct thy paths.
—Proverbs 3:5 – 6 KJV

My parents were in their late seventies. Daddy was my Rock of Gibraltar. Being the youngest child and only daughter, I had always been Daddy's little girl. Sure, he had undergone serious major surgery, but he miraculously pulled through. Sure, he had Parkinson's, and with each visit home he seemed more frail. But I refused to accept the harsh reality that my rock was crumbling.

Mother faithfully took care of Daddy. But then she started complaining she couldn't think of the right word to say when conversing. She seemed more frustrated when trying to prepare meals. But I ignored the signals that something was wrong.

I wrote my parents frequently, called often, and always asked, "How are you?"

Daddy would succinctly respond, "Oh, we're fine."

Then one day the phone rang. A friend said, "Betty,

your mother is regressing mentally. I'm concerned. I think you need to make a trip home."

My husband, Earl, is much better with crisis situations and problem-solving than I, so he flew to Kansas City. Mother, Daddy, and he made the unanimous decision that something needed to be done. But what? Mom and Dad really weren't bad enough to go to a nursing home, yet they were going to need help with activities of daily living.

Earl called that evening. "What would you think of moving them in with us?" he asked.

Without hesitation I replied, "I'd love it." Our two children agreed they would enjoy having their grandparents live with them. And so we all willingly enlisted in the great army of people caring for aging parents and grandparents. But nothing in the basic training of life prepared us for what was ahead.

Until then words such as ostomy, foley, Duoderm dressing, decubitus ulcer, dementia, and incontinence were irrelevant entries in Webster's dictionary. Soon after, definitions erupted into reality.

Until then items such as bathtub safety rails, transfer benches, deluxe portable commodes, folding walkers, flotation cushions, Depend shields, safety vests, and ostomy pouches were products in a medical catalog. Now they all occupied my home.

Until then I was free to set my own schedule. Now, ready or not, my entire life revolved around pill schedules, bathroom needs, doctors' appointments, and the myriad concerns involved in caring for aging parents. After the initial excitement faded, I cried, "God, how are we going to handle this? I know nothing about caring for aging parents."

As I prayed for wisdom, God brought to my mind a story in 2 Chronicles, chapter 20. A vast army was advancing on Israel. Jehoshaphat begged the Lord for help: "We don't know what to do, but we are looking to you" (v. 12 TLB). God replied, "Don't be afraid or discouraged . . . for the Lord is with you" (v. 17 TLB).

During the next four years of caregiving, we frequently spread our problems out before the Lord. "We don't know what to do," we told Him. Without fail, He directed our paths.

Father, we trust You to guide us in the way of wisdom. Thank You for providing the needed daily strength for our caregiving responsibilities.

—**Betty Benson Robertson**

BLESSED

ASSURANCE

Fear thou not; for I am with thee: be not dismayed; for
I am thy God: I will strengthen thee.
—Isaiah 41:10 KJV

My mother lived with my husband and me because my father had deserted her. She had quite a hearing loss, but she loved to read and study her Bible. In former years she had taught adult Sunday school classes. She still often led a Bible study or gave a devotion for the women's auxiliary of the nearby rescue mission. That mission was dear to her heart for she always prayed that sometime, somewhere, my father might be led to go to such a place and finally accept the Lord Jesus as his Savior.

Mother also loved to sew. She did beautiful needlework and made all of her own clothes. At times, though, Mother grew despondent because of the rejection she naturally felt from her husband leaving her. And special days like my father's birthday, their anniversary, and even her own birthday, were hard for her.

As the years went by, Mother began to have a lot more difficulty with hearing and her sight began to dim. Even though she was a woman of great faith, she sometimes became frustrated. How was she going to read her Bible? How was she going to sew? What could she do with her time?

Mother still insisted that washing the dishes was her job. She objected to me helping her. I knew she needed to be needed so I let her be. She became more withdrawn and often wondered why the Lord didn't take her home.

One day when we were talking together, Mother seemed to have a faraway look in her eyes. Slowly she said, "I wonder how your Dad died? I can't seem to recall anything about it anymore."

I stood there in a state of shock, wondering how to answer. After a bit she went on to speak about something else totally unrelated to her question. There was no need for me to say anything. Mother never spoke of my dad again. And the Lord did take her home to be with Him, just before her ninety-first birthday.

Father God, thank You that I know Mother is safely with You.

—**Betty C. Stevens**

ॐ

PUTTING LIFE
IN A BOX

*If I give all my property bit by bit
and if I hand over my body in order to boast,
and I don't have love, I gain nothing.*
—1 Corinthians 13:3 (author's translation)

My husband and I were only in our twenties when my widowed mother-in-law began experiencing the first stages of Alzheimer's. She began forgetting to take her medicine to stabilize her high blood pressure. *How long*, we wondered, *could she survive without the proper medication?*

My husband had recently buried his father. He was worried about losing his mother too. His fidgety sleep woke me nightly. I talked to him, prayed for him, and sought the Lord's answer.

"Honey, let's sell the house and move in with Mom," I said one day. "Then you wouldn't worry about her so much."

"Do you really mean it?" he asked, amazed.

"Sure, it'd be better to move in with Mom than to have you worry like this," I admitted.

"Do you think it would work with our kids and all?"

"Well, it's got to be better than the way we're living now," I surmised.

After arrangements were made, our house sold in two days. My husband and I, our two young children, and our cat moved in with Mom.

The transition seemed smooth—at first. Mom's palatial home could accommodate us, but it couldn't handle our possessions stored away in boxes. I found myself missing my knickknack shelf and those little things that brought joy. I was annoyed that we got the smallest bedroom with its ugly secondhand green antiqued bedroom set Mom had purchased.

I began to resent the loss of my house. More than that, I began to resent the loss of my freedom and my identity as a married grown woman. Along with my stuff in boxes, I seemed to have placed my status as an adult. Although parents ourselves, my husband and I had become children once more.

"Lord, I gave away our row home to help out, but now I'm being asked to give away myself," I frequently grumbled during that time of adjustment or, more honestly, resentment.

One day He pointed me to 1 Corinthians 13:3. I had given all my possessions along with some of my body as evidenced by my loss of status and freedom. But the purpose, He reminded me, was for love and with love. Through the struggle came the grace to accept what it cost me personally to help Mom. It was then I found I had

110

love—love for Mom despite her limitations, and love for my young family resilient enough to help Mom during this time of her life.

Dear Lord, thank You for reminding me that nothing I can give can be selfless without Your grace.

—Karen L. Onesti

R o l e   R e v e r s a l

Now I'm the "mommy,"
And you are the child
Tripping and spilling,
Emotions run wild
At the least inconvenience.
You can't understand.
Who can respond
To such constant demand?
Jesus replies,
"In My strength, child,
You can."

—Barbara A. Walk

ON BEING
PARENTED

He will renew your life and sustain you in your old age.
—Ruth 4:15 NIV

Fifteen years ago our daughter, Verda, and her husband, Homer, moved from their ranch house to a spacious farmhouse with their three young children. It had been converted into two apartments plus living quarters for the owner.

I asked Verda, "What changes are you going to make?"

"We'll remodel," she said. "I want the whole house for our family. Then we'll have room for you and Dad when you need it."

Oh, really! I thought, as this was far from my mind. I was happy in my work in our school district. My husband was a semi-retired farmer.

But time pushed us onward. Multiplied years and unexpected illnesses took their toll. Now their house seems empty, their children grown and gone. Several months ago, without forethought, I casually said to Verda, "Will you have room for us after awhile? We would pay for remodeling and give you something monthly."

"Of course," she answered quickly. Then she paused and added, "But I'll need to talk it over with Homer and get back to you."

Knowing her father was recovering from another hospital stay, Verda didn't waste any time. She soon phoned and said it was okay with Homer. His brother, a building contractor, will do the work. They plan for a bedroom, a kitchen with sunporch, and a living room. A bath is already in place.

They will accept as a gift our payment for the remodeling, the kitchen installation being the major expenditure. They will not charge us anything monthly, though we plan to pay for our utilities and phone. "This is not rental property," they insist, "but for family."

As we spent time in the rooms one day, I threw out this hint, "I can picture you two living here someday. Please plan it to suit yourselves."

My daughter answered, "I've thought of that. When you don't need it, we can sell the house to one of our children and live here. Our roles will be reversed then."

After we sign the contract and the work is started, we will sell our home and some personal property. This forty-mile move, this uprooting, will not be easy for us. My husband, Alvin, always has lived within five miles of his birthplace. We have been here a long time, but we want to dispose of our property while we are able or someone else will need to do it for us. So now, I am sorting and packing.

Thank You, heavenly Father, for children that renew and sustain. May their tribe increase.

—Edna Mast

Gaining Through Loss

All of life is loss,
And we must count the cost
Of giving up what we have loved
Into the care of God above.
Our friends, our hopes, our fears, our plans—
And place them in His loving hands.
His way for us is always best,
And we need only learn to rest
Each day within His holy will,
And hear His words, "Peace, be still."

—Josie Halbert

WAIT
FOR ME

"Your care for others is the measure of your greatness."
—Luke 9:48 TLB

I awoke at 4:00 A.M. and tiptoed downstairs, intending to boot up the computer and start writing. But then I remembered this advice: "Before you begin writing, wait before the Lord. Ask Him what to write about."

"Uh-oh, Lord! There I go again, plunging into my own agenda, without waiting for Your direction. I'm sorry. What do You want me to write about?"

"Waiting for your mother."

"Oh, dear, Lord, You touched a sore spot. I've been feeling guilty lately because I haven't been waiting for Mother while she finishes eating, dressing, washing . . . And I've been getting irritated too. Of course, I know it isn't even common courtesy. But Lord, You know I'm always in high gear, and Mother's in low . . . or reverse! She probably doesn't even realize I'm not there. Maybe she doesn't mind being left to finish alone."

"Yes, she does realize. She minds. And you are making her feel uncomfortable and in the way."

"I'm sorry, Lord. I guess I've been caring more about my time and interests than how Mother feels. That's not good caregiving. Forgive me. Please help me slow down and wait for her."

"Remember when you were young? You always got a pain in your side from running. You never could keep up with the other children. Remember how it felt, having to call out, 'Wait for me?'"

"Thank You for that reminder, Lord. I felt miserable when they left me behind!

"Mmm. It's hard to carry on a conversation with Mother 'cause she often loses the words. But while I wait with her, I can pray. Maybe slowing down and waiting for Mother will be good for me. Maybe it will even lower my blood pressure.

"You're smiling now, aren't You, Lord?"

Dear heavenly Father, thank You for speaking with me this morning. Help me wait . . . for You, and for Mother, with a humble spirit.

—**Jean M. Olsen**

REACHING ACROSS

THE GENERATIONS

Even when I am old and gray,
do not forsake me, O God,
till I declare your power to the next generation,
your might to all who are to come.
—Psalm 71:18 NIV

The phone rang for the second time that morning.

"It's Dad. He's gone . . ." My mother's voice trailed off.

Just a half hour before, my mother had called to tell me she had taken Dad to the hospital but that he was fine. Now God had called him home.

Out of concern for Mom, I tried to swallow my own grief. "I'm coming, Mama," I cried. "I'll be there as soon as I can."

Blindly I made my way to the hospital forty miles away to be with my mother. For as long as I could remember, Mom was always there to soothe away my hurts. She'd hold me, stroke my head, and sing comforting words into my ear until I was able to face the world again.

Now it was I who held her. As I put my arms around

her, I could feel how thin and frail she'd become from five years of worrying about and caring for Dad. She was no longer the strong, capable, manager of the home; the one who could heal all hurts; the one who had a practical solution for everything. For the time being, she was the hurting child; a child who needed someone to care for her and help her heal. In that moment, I realized that Mother and I had switched roles and I had become the parent.

I took charge, making funeral arrangements, cooking, taking care of Mom's business, clearing out and selling the house she and Dad had shared. Then I took her home to live with me and my family.

Though Mom quickly recovered, she never gained the confidence to live alone. In many ways I still function as the parent, but she has an unquenchable spirit and a quiet, unshakable faith. She lives out her days witnessing to God's power "to the next generation"—blessing my husband and me, our children and our grandchildren — declaring God's might "to all who are to come."

Lord, we thank You for the loving witness of Your elderly saints which reaches across generations.

—**June Eaton**

SALT

ON MUFFINS

*I refresh the humble and give new courage
to those with repentant hearts.*
—Isaiah 57:15 TLB

Oh, I'm so glad you're finally up. I've been sitting here for hours all by myself," Mom said as she threw her arms around me and hugged me.

I could feel her trembling and feel myself getting defensive. "You should have stayed in bed longer," I said. "It's only 8:00 A.M. And it's a Saturday!"

"Well, I don't know what day it is. I'm sorry," she said, but her voice sounded more accusing than apologetic.

I walked into the kitchen and began preparing homemade muffins for breakfast. I measured the flour, sugar, baking powder, and salt into the bowl as Mom talked nonstop. As usual, she wasn't making a lot of sense and, as usual, I was only half listening and half paying attention to what I was doing.

"Oh, no," I groaned.

"What's wrong?" Mother asked.

"My muffins!"

119

"What did you do?"

"I added three teaspoons of salt instead of one."

"They'll be fine, dear. Some people put salt on muffins anyway."

"No, Mother. You don't put salt on muffins." I tried spooning out the salt but I couldn't tell if I was getting salt or sugar.

"It's my fault," she said. "I was talking too much. I'll leave you alone." Her shoulders slumped more than usual as she turned and walked away.

I tried to tell her it wasn't her fault, but it didn't help ease her pain or my guilt.

The morning went downhill from there. Getting Mom dressed was a bigger chore than usual. I just about had to wrestle her out of the slip and dress she had put on over her nightgown. Then I discovered she was wearing four pairs of undies to "keep warm."

Convincing her that she didn't need to wear her boots in the house was another problem. "Please stop arguing with me," I finally screeched. The guilts attacked me again.

"God, I'm sorry. I just can't do it. Please help me," I pleaded when I finally grabbed a few minutes alone for Bible study and prayer. His answer came in a verse I hadn't discovered before: "I refresh the humble and give new courage to those with repentant hearts" (Isa. 57:15 TLB).

Thank You, God, for Your forgiveness and for Your strength to keep on keeping on in a role that isn't easy.

—Marlene Bagnull

Bits and Pieces

There are bits and pieces of my mind
That I've misplaced from time to time.
Some are scattered, here and there,
Goodness gracious, do I know where?
Beside the sofa, on the stair,
Probably under my favorite chair!
The envelope stamped with no address,
One lonely earring, now laid to rest.
My favorite recipe hides from me,
What on earth will the next thing be?
If you find some pieces,
Greatly treasured by me,
Please handle them gently
And return C.O.D.

—Alice Everett Schock

HIDDEN

IN DARKNESS

Where could I go to escape from you?
Where could I get away from your presence?
If I went up to heaven, you would be there;
if I lay down in the world of the dead,
you would be there.
—Psalm 139:7–8 TEV

As I helped Mom into her nightgown, I was smiling, remembering the pleasant evening. Mom had sat with me and my husband contentedly stitching quilt blocks together. I allowed myself to drift along in the happy illusion that all was well. The illusion shattered when I gently kissed her velvet cheek and started to close the bedroom door.

She jerked upright on the bed. "Where are you going? It's late. It's past your bedtime."

"I'm going to bed, Mom," I assured her. "If you need me, I'll be right across the hall."

Her familiar, beloved face changed into something ugly and frightening as she narrowed her eyes and spat at me, "You're sleeping with *that man,* aren't you!"

I went to her and put my arm around her shoulders. "Mom, Ron is my husband. We've been married for a long, long time."

She pushed me away and began slapping at me. "You're lying to me! I've never seen that man before!" Her voice was shrill.

I eased her back onto the pillow, turning my face away from her wildly flailing arms. I wanted to stroke her, hoping somehow to calm her, but her body was rigid. She lurched out of my reach.

Her eyes darted back and forth, and she clawed at her face. I knew I had lost her once again to some unknown nightmare world of terror. Tears brimmed over as I prayed, "God, give me the love to bring her back to the gentle, sweet person who was my mom."

Even as I prayed, I knew my love wasn't enough. There was no way for me to reach into that terrible darkness where Mom sometimes lost herself. But then the familiar words of Psalm 139 filtered into my mind, "but even darkness is not dark for you, and the night is as bright as the day" (v. 12 TEV).

The vise of grief and fear that gripped me eased a little. My love could not reach Mom, but God's love could. There is no place too dark, no place too far away, that His child can be lost from Him.

Loving Father, I am trusting that You are surrounding Mom on every side, protecting her with Your love.
—Lyn Jackson

Be Still

Be still, My child, and know that I am God,
The everlasting Counselor and King.
Receive the comfort of My staff and rod,
And all your cares and burdens to Me bring.
Lift up your eyes unto the hills above,
And find the peace and help I long to give.
Be ever mindful of My gracious love,
And know that by My power you shall live.
For in the day you sought Me, I was found,
And in the day you called, I heard your prayer.
And when at night you wept, I heard the sound
And wiped away the tears of your despair.
Be still, My child, and know that I am He
Who holds you in His heart eternally.

—**Mary Ann L. Diorio**

TODAY IS
THE DAY

This is the day which the LORD hath made;
we will rejoice and be glad in it.
—Psalm 118:24 KJV

I still remember the jolt I received a few years ago when my youngest daughter asked, "Will you be glad when I'm gone?" She was only returning to college after Christmas vacation, but her question triggered some serious thought. Would I be glad when she went back to college? Would I be relieved when she left our nest permanently?

I suppose every parent sometimes looks ahead to the next phase of his child's life when things will be a little easier, less demanding. Although bringing up children is a delightful, exciting experience, it comes with a bundle of hassles, sometimes even horrors. But when I measured the hassles against the joy of her presence, there was no contest. Her presence won. Later, when she was twenty-five and the time was right, she left us to build her own nest, with mutual agreement and blessing.

Two years before our daughter moved out, my mother moved in. This eighty-nine-year-old "child" isn't maturing and preparing to leave the nest. Just the opposite. She's losing skills, a little at a time.

The mantle of humble, unselfish, gentle caregiver doesn't fit me. But it's the one God has lovingly, wisely, placed on my shoulders for today. Only by His grace can I behave in such a way that Mother will never look at me and ask, "Will you be glad when I'm gone?"

So when I'm feeling grumpy, I think of all Mother did for me when I was a child. She must have wished a thousand times that I would grow up and stop waking her in the middle of the night with leg aches or nosebleeds. But while they lasted, she was there to willingly rub my legs with Absorbine Jr. and clean up after my bloody nose.

Before Jesus went to the cross, He asked His Father, if possible, to take the cup from Him. I've asked God the same thing, but so far His answer has been: "You are to help your [mother] until the LORD gives [her] rest ... After that, you may go back and occupy your own land" (Josh. 1:15 NIV).

Lord God, help me not to spend so much time dreaming about some easier tomorrow, that I miss Your blessing today.

—Jean M. Olsen

HEALED

WOUNDS

*And be kind to one another, tenderhearted, forgiving
one another, even as God in Christ forgave you.*
—Ephesians 4:32 NKJV

My in-laws hadn't always been kind to my children and
me—not intentionally, they simply had favorites and we
weren't among them. I thought I'd buried the hurts when
my mother-in-law came to stay with us after her husband
passed away. I honestly thought so, until the morning of
that first day.

My twenty-year-old daughter sat at the kitchen table
staring into her black coffee. "I'm sorry, Mom," she said,
not raising her eyes from the cup. "She never gave me a
second thought all the while I was growing up. I'm not
about to fall all over her now." Pushing herself away from
the table she left the room.

Without warning, unpleasant memories from the early
years of my marriage surfaced.

"This is *our* granddaughter," my mother-in-law had
once said as she picked up my niece, ignoring my daughter

as she stood in anticipation of attention. She got none. That hurt!

"Johnny's grandma is coming up the driveway!" my youngest son had called, referring to his cousin. That hurt, because it was his grandma too!

All the bitter feelings of unfairness surfaced. With a wounded spirit I took them to the Lord.

"Remember when . . ." I told Him one incident after another, confident I had every right to my bitterness.

He said, "Forgive her."

"But she's not sorry. She'd do the same thing over again if she had the chance."

He said, "Forgive her."

"But, Lord . . ."

"You can't carry that sin of unforgiveness into My throne room," He said. "Forgive her."

"Lord," I cried, "You don't understand." But in my spirit I heard His voice echoing through the valley of the shadow of His death, from Golgotha's Hill: "Father, forgive them; for they know not what they do" (Luke 23:34 KJV).

Oh, yes, He understood. And He knew nothing she had ever done or said was worth the distance my unforgiveness would put between Him and me.

Reluctantly, I laid my stubborn heart upon His altar not knowing how, or if, I could forgive. How great God is! He gave my heart back to me, healed and forgiving.

Lord, I thank You for every unpleasant memory that has become a healed wound. Like the scars in Your hands, they remind me of the forgiveness I received at the Cross. Because of that cross I can forgive those who sin against me. The burden of bitterness is gone, and in its place reigns the peace that passes understanding.

—Sandra Forster

C h o i c e

The pain is real, Lord.
I have good reason to feel this way—
trying, waiting, striving, failing . . .
Hate!
It's my right.
Yet—in the stillness of my soul
a voice;
a quiet voice . . .
barely audible
but speaking louder than the pain.
"Love—
It's My command."

—Marcia Krugh Leaser

⍺

THE FIRST

LIGHT OF DAWN

*Then your light will break forth like the dawn,
and your healing will quickly appear.*
—Isaiah 58:8 NIV

J anet, can you hear me? Janet! I can't sleep!"

It had started about four A.M., again. She thought she was whispering, but it resounded like a shout throughout my aching, sleep-starved mind.

"Isn't it time for breakfast? You know, I need to take my insulin on schedule. My legs are hurting again. Are you going to take me to the doctor today? He'll make them feel better. He always makes them feel better."

There was no use trying to explain that it was Saturday, hours before breakfast time. She no longer understood the concept of time. And she was afraid of the dark.

All night she tried to spare me, muttering over and over, "I'd better wait a bit. Is it time yet? Maybe I'd better wait a bit."

She was getting louder now. How could I keep her from rousing the entire household?

"Come on, Mom. Let's go for a ride."

I went to get her teeth, her favorite sweater, her purse. Then I searched for my purse and the car keys.

Finally, we were ready for the trek through the kitchen and living room, across the porch, and down the steps to the car. Once settled in the car, the questions began again.

"Are you taking me to the doctor? When are we going to have breakfast? Are you going to feed me today?"

As we drove through the dark countryside, my thoughts whirled. *At least the others will get a good night's sleep. Maybe I can catch a couple hours after they're up to keep an eye on her.*

Suddenly, quiet engulfed me. A glance showed me that she was still awake, staring across the fields at a narrow band of pink showing on the horizon.

"Oh, look," she whispered. "I think the sun's coming up." And so it was.

We kept driving into the east, watching the pink band widen, the light chasing away the darkness until, with a flash, the sky turned golden and then blue as the sun rose above the horizon.

"Well," Mom sighed, her face shining, "guess it's time for breakfast now, huh?"

"Yes, Mom, I guess it is," I agreed. As I turned to smile at her, her eyelids closed and her head sank back against the seat. Once again the sun was up. All was right with Mom's world.

Dear Father God, thank You for those special moments

131

of peace in the middle of strife. Help us to hang on to that
peace in spite of the turmoil around us.

—**Janet Milano Ihle**

T h r e a d s   o f   H e r e d i t y

I am so tired, Lord.
Please let him sleep longer this time.
Please help me go back to sleep more quickly.
You know I have to get up at six.
I wonder if Grandma prayed this same prayer
Ninety years ago just after his birth.
How much have I inherited from her?
I need her patience, her faith,
Her calm acceptance of Your will.
Help me pick up the threads
Of my heredity, Lord.
Help me follow my grandmother's footsteps,
Finding my strength in You.

—**Helen Kammerdiener**

EVER

PRESENT

*God is our refuge and strength,
a very present help in trouble.*
—Psalm 46:1 KJV

"T ara," Dad called in desperation. "Come here, I need you!"

I rolled my eyes as I walked toward his bedroom. All of the doctors confirmed that there was nothing physically wrong with Dad. Yet day after day he laid in bed convinced he was dying. Mental illness immobilized his body and spirit.

I sat on the edge of his bed, fighting resentment. Throughout my childhood, Dad was never there when I needed him most, but now he expected so much from me.

"What's wrong, Dad?" I asked impatiently.

He held his chest and grimaced. "A pain in my chest," he huffed, gasping for air. "Take me to the emergency room!"

Weeks earlier, his psychiatrist assured us that he was experiencing nothing more than panic attacks. This was

133

the second attack in two days—the third trip to the hospital in one week.

"Take deep breaths," I insisted. "It'll pass."

"No! Something's wrong," he snapped.

My intolerance mingled with guilt. What if something was really wrong? I helped Dad to the car and raced toward the hospital. On the way, Dad moaned, his face gaunt and pale, his eyes wet with tears.

I wanted to chastise him. I wanted to abandon him. Instead, I prayed, "God, please help me."

Suddenly, I realized that Dad's false symptoms were very real to him. My heart filled with love and compassion as I reached to squeeze his hand. "Don't worry, Dad. You'll be okay."

And in that moment, Dad's voice broke as he spoke words I had never heard him say before. "I love you, Tara. . . . I don't know what I would do without you."

I swallowed hard and blinked back the tears as unspoken forgiveness flowed. Our heavenly Father was present for both Dad and me in our greatest time of need. Still clutching his hand, I whispered my praise to God. "I love you, too, Dad."

Father God, though we often fail the ones we love, You never fail us when we need You the most. Thank You for being such a loving and helpful heavenly Father.

—**Tara Martin**

MINING

THE GOLD

I praise you for remembering me in everything and for holding to the teachings, just as I passed them on to you.
—1 Corinthians 11:2 NIV

Mother was spending her last years in my home battling cancer. She stared into space as she reclined on her lounger. I sat at her feet to call her back from her mental meandering.

"Do you know something that bothers me?" I asked in an effort to divert her thoughts and get her talking.

"What's that?" She did perk up a little bit.

"Well, even though Christ is very real to me today, and has been for years, I can't remember when I actually became a Christian," I stated.

"Oh, I remember that well. You were only eight years old when you knelt in prayer and asked the Lord's forgiveness," Mother responded.

Can you imagine my excitement at learning the answer to a question that had plagued me almost all of my life? I suddenly realized the gold mine of memories that my mother held in her heart and mind.

How blessed I was to be able to listen to Mother reminisce and tell some stories that I'd never heard before. History became alive as we mined the gold buried in her memory bank. I listened with both ears as I cared for her.

Did you ever forget something vitally important? Who hasn't. Sometimes we try to blame it on old age, but forgetfulness isn't limited to the elderly. Seniors who are ill and have nothing to do but sit and think are a precious resource for memories.

If we had not taken time to chat that first time, I'd have never known when Christ really touched my heart. I'll always be grateful for those few precious moments, as well as for the learning sessions that followed.

Even though some tales may be told repeatedly, the better for us to remember them and pass them on. Family histories, including spiritual journeys, can knit us all closer together.

Father, help us as we listen to the gold being mined from the hearts of our loved ones. Help us to remember these precious moments, to cherish them, and to pass them on.

—Grayce L. Weibley

THE
LORD'S HOUSE

I was glad when they said unto me,
Let us go into the house of the LORD.
—Psalm 122:1 KJV

After devoting forty years to building up the inner-city church we attended, my father retired, moved to a rural suburb, and never went to church again. At a time when he needed the most support, he lost touch with his biggest support group—his church. When he died, a stranger delivered his eulogy. Mostly strangers attended his funeral.

I grieved for him, remembering how deeply involved he had been in the work of the church and how he had faithfully transported my brothers and me a long distance to our church. He made church activities an important part of our lives.

At Dad's funeral, I determined that Mom was not going to suffer the same fate. She was going to be surrounded by people who knew and appreciated her. The following Sunday, and all of the Sundays since, I have made sure she got to church.

"How I've missed all of this," she said, brushing away

a tear on her first Sunday back. Now the sparkle has returned to her eyes. At eighty-six, she not only attends worship services, she takes part in Bible studies and helps make quilts with the sewing circle. On Sundays after worship, she gives and receives dozens of hugs. When she goes to be with the Lord, she will be missed by many.

It's so easy to rationalize and say, "I'm a good Christian. Mom's a good Christian. It's too much trouble to go to church today. We'll just have our prayer and devotions at home." But the truth is, both Mom and I need the blessings of church attendance as long as it is physically possible. No matter how inconvenient, we need to maintain contact with the Body of Christ, need to be refreshed by the healing words of the Bible, and need to feel the presence of the Lord in His house.

I'll always be grateful to both my parents for bringing me to the Lord's house. Now that our roles are reversed, I'm simply following their example.

Lord, thank You for mothers and fathers who have faithfully brought their children to the Lord's house. As we become parents to our parents, help us to remember our roots and to carry on our legacy.

—June Eaton

FROM WEAKNESS
TOWARD STRENGTH

My days are like a shadow that declineth;
and I am withered like grass.
But thou, O LORD, shalt endure for ever.
—Psalm 102:11–12 KJV

I can't make it, honey."

She looks drawn, disheveled, particularly vulnerable with the post-implant shield taped over her left eye. Her words sound plausible. But she *has* to make it—not only because of her appointment with her ophthalmologist, but because my world depends on her "making it" as she has for the past ninety-two years. She has survived and surmounted crises big and small. Now, for the first time, my heart congeals with the admission that some morning she may not make it.

Is it this knowledge which sharpens my voice, then fills me with shame as I gently support her shambling progress to the kitchen? Perhaps, as experts suggest, her obvious mortality forces me to face my own. Am I that selfish? That shallow? That lacking in faith? "You'll feel better once you've eaten," I assure her—and myself.

My husband has already poured her coffee. A banana and paring knife wait beside the steaming cup. Halfheartedly, she begins the breakfast ritual, cutting the fruit into equal parts and pushing one half toward him. This morning, however, she makes no smiling comment. She picks at her cereal. Refuses toast. But, surely I'm not imagining, she's sitting somewhat straighter. Any moment, now, she'll ask what time we need to go.

I consider her stalwart faith through the deaths of four young children; how, for all our sakes, she survived decades of asthma only through prayer and twenty shots of Adrenalin, self-administered, each day; how, for twenty-eight years after my father's death, she lived alone. Of course, she'll make it! *Can't* is a word she's never acknowledged.

I help her to her room. Sighing, she leans heavily on support she often rejects. "How soon," she asks quaveringly, "do we have to leave?"

And inwardly I praise God. Just as I knew! She's going to make it . . . this time.

Father God, help us to look beyond the inevitabilities of this world to the promise of eternal life and wholeness in Your presence.

—**Evelyn Minshull**

&

PLEASE, LORD,

NOT TODAY!

When I am weak, then I am strong—the less I have,
the more I depend on him.
—2 Corinthians 12:10 TLB

We were holding a Missions Conference at church, and I had agreed to cook dinner for the guest speaker and his wife. I had planned my day carefully, but everything had gone wrong. Most frustrating of all, Mom had reacted to my tension by becoming more difficult than usual. Still, as I sprinted through the house dusting and straightening up, it looked as if I might make it. With half an hour before my guests were due to arrive, I showered hastily and threw on a robe. Just one quick check on Mom and then I would get dressed. As I opened the bathroom door, I saw a trail of clothes from Mom's bedroom into the living room. "Oh, no, Lord," I gasped. "Please, not today!"

I ran to the living room and found things strewn everywhere. Mom was packing again! With mounting panic, I grabbed up shoes and a pile of clothes. Had Mom emptied her whole closet?

Mom was peering out the front window. "When are they going to come? Daddy told me he'd get me today."

"Mom, your parents aren't coming. Now take all this stuff back to your room. Remember, we're having guests?" I managed to keep my voice calm.

Mom didn't seem to hear. She twisted her apron around her wrinkled hands. "They should be here by now. It's getting dark. We've got to get home."

I took a deep breath. "Lord, give me the patience and the time to deal with this," I whispered. Then I gathered Mom into my arms. "Your parents have been with God for a very long time. Someday soon you will go to heaven to be with them. But it won't be today. And you won't need to pack. God will have everything you need waiting for you."

As always, Mom was at first shocked and then angry. The tears came and she shuffled to her bedroom, slamming the door behind her.

As I slipped into my dress, I could hear the banging of dresser drawers. I knew Mom was pulling out more things, talking to herself in a litany of despair. "I won't be ready when they come. I've got to get packed. I don't want them to leave me here. I want to go home."

I sank down on my knees by the bed. "Sometimes it's so hard, Lord. My days are too full. I feel so rushed. Please get me through this evening."

A sense of peace came over me. Everything would be okay. I had prayed before offering my hospitality, and I believed I was in the Lord's will. If He was to have the glory, then I must let Him fight the battle.

Thank You, Lord, for Your promise that Your power is greatest when I am weak.

— **Twyla Wilson as told to Lyn Jackson**

S t r e n g t h   f o r   M y   D a y

Uncertainties around me flow,
  My sky is overcast,
But this one certainty I know—
  These troubles will not last
Beyond my Father's care and love;
  For nothing will be mine
That can't be used by God above
  As part of His design.
So I give Him each trying day—
  Severity and length
Are not my chief concern—I pray
  That God will be my strength.

— **Merna B. Shank**

Childproof Latches

Early morning.
Eyes barely focused I stumble down the steps.
There is Mother in my kitchen,
doing my dishes—again.
I groan, knowing what I'll find
in the cabinets and drawers.
Smeary glasses, dirty dishes,
knives, forks, and spoons—jumbled.

Childproof latches did not work.
She opened them.
Demented—but stubborn as ever.
Determined, she watched
and practiced and figured
every drawer, every cabinet,
every lock but one.

And then that, too, with God's help,
swinging wide my heart to blessings.
I see my mother with new eyes.
Alive—whispering with each dirty dish
and jumbled drawer:
Please let me help.
Please let me clean.
Please let me love you—again.

—Marlene Bagnull

A BUNCH OF
GOBBLEDYGOOK!

*A merry heart
makes a cheerful countenance.*
—Proverbs 15:13 NKJV

Oh, Don," my mother-in-law gasped, "that's just a bunch of gobbledygook!"

Grace had come to live with us when she was eighty-seven years old and, though she could not imagine it, her thinking was almost totally confused. One day as we ate lunch together, I could feel her agitation. She tapped her fingers and stared into space. "Where are you, Mom?" I asked.

"I'm trying to figure out how he dumped me for you."

Don tried to explain that he was her son and my husband. She just shook her head, unconvinced. Finally, he drew a family tree on paper for her. "You married my dad and had me. Anne's parents married one another and had Anne. Then Anne and I married and had our children. See?"

Mom looked up from the paper and said those unforgettable words: "Oh, Don, that's just a bunch of gobbledygook! If the whole world were run like that, what a mess it would be!"

Amusing, yes, but behind those words were her frustration at finding her daughter-in-law caring for her. I understood that. Although we were fond of one another, there had been tension and conflict in the past because we both loved the same man.

Don's father died when he was four. Mom invested herself totally in Don. Now she thought he was her husband. One day she confided the shocking truth to her sister: "He kisses me goodnight and goes to bed with her!"

What to do? We had to allow ourselves the freedom to laugh, not at her, but privately, because it was truly funny. We also had to honor her by being sensitive to her feelings. I was grateful to her for the fine man she had raised. She had been brave and independent raising him alone during the Great Depression. I recognized her bewilderment at being dependent on me and so I prayed for her.

Dear Lord, give me grace to care for Grace as though I were caring for You. Help me to be patient and understanding. And thank You, Lord, for a good sense of humor!
—**Anne H. Gross**

HE THAT IS GREATEST,
LET HIM SERVE

*And the King shall answer and say unto them, Verily I
say unto you, Inasmuch as ye have done it unto one of
the least of these my brethren, ye have done it unto me.*
—Matthew 25:40 KJV

As I took the aqua basin from its plastic bag and prepared
to soak my father's ulcerated foot, I felt somewhat depressed. Six years ago we had moved my father into our
newly-remodeled living room. We had no spare bedroom
downstairs, and he couldn't climb stairs or take care of
himself at home. In order to adequately care for Dad, we
had to delay laying our new carpet and furnishing the living
room. This didn't bother my father, but I must admit I
chafed under the circumstances.

I was feeling a bit sorry for myself that bright March
Sunday morning. It was Easter, but I had to stay home from
church to care for my aged father.

I sighed. I could see the whole scene. Lilies and palms
banked the altar. Frills and ruffles adorned the ladies'
spring outfits. Triumphant hymns filled the sanctuary. A
stirring sermon voiced the meaning of Easter. But I would

miss all of this as I stayed home to take care of my ninety-two-year-old father who nearly lost a leg due to a gangrenous ulcer a few months ago. His foot required a daily soaking, dressing, and wrapping.

As I took the towel and lowered the basin to his foot, my mind traveled back to a foot-washing scene just a few short days before the first Easter. It was as though a voice inside me said, "Which celebration of Easter is more important to me?"

I remembered the words of Jesus to His disciples at their last meal together: "He that is greatest among you, let him be . . . as he that doth serve" (Luke 22:26 KJV).

I knew the answer. My burden lifted and I knew that as I washed my father's feet, I was in reality washing my Savior's. Could I do anything more important? I felt peace as I looked up from my kneeling position at my father's feet into the eyes of both my earthly and my heavenly Father.

Father, I thank You for Your sustaining presence through those years ministering to me as I ministered to my father.

—**June Gilbaugh**

FINDING
FAULT

*And let us not grow weary while doing good, for in due
season we shall reap if we do not lose heart.*
—Galatians 6:9 NKJV

In caring for my mother the last few months of her life,
the reversal of roles was one of the most difficult things
for me to cope with. When I was a child, Mom had washed
my face, combed my hair, and dressed me. Now I was
doing that for her.

Perhaps it wouldn't have been so hard had her patient
and pleasant manner remained. Yet, as her fearfulness and
apprehension about her health grew, so did her frustration
at having to be waited on and not being able to do things
for herself.

Some days Mom would be appreciative of every little
thing. Other days she found fault with everything I did. At
the end of such days, I would often be in tears.

Then I consulted my sister who stayed with Mom one
day a week so that I could shop and get out of the house.
"Does Mom criticize the way you do things for her?" I
inquired.

"Does she ever," my sister, Helen, responded. "She complains, 'Why can't you do it the way your sister does?' That includes everything from the way I make her bed to the way I comb her hair!"

At that, I burst into laughter and explained to my puzzled sister, "Why, Helen, she says the very same things to me!"

Mom didn't mean to be disagreeable. She wasn't angry with me or with Helen. What was really bothering her was the fact that she had to be dependent on us.

Thank You, Father God, for the strength You give each day and for Your promise that, as our days, so shall our strength be.

—**Delores Elaine Bius**

H e   N e v e r   L e a v e s   U s

God promises not to leave us
Nor forsake us from His care,
Yet at times it seems He's absent,
That He really is not there.
It seems that He is silent,
Hidden from our view,
Yet truly He is always there,
Helping to see us through.

—**Frances Gregory Pasch**

DISSOLVED

IN LAUGHTER

Our mouths were filled with laughter.
—Psalm 126:2 NIV

Humor, wonderful humor, was a gift given to my mom and her side of the family. They are just funny and fun-loving persons. After a few hours with them, your jaw often hurts from so much laughter.

No matter how serious a situation would be, my mother would find some humor in it. I can remember getting annoyed with her at times because she refused to be "just" sad, serious, or sullen. Her talent for humor would seek out a comical side to crisis. When her memory started to fade, she'd make us laugh at her forgetfulness.

One day I prepared a bath for her. I also prepared a "soak" for her false teeth. When she got out of the tub and dried off, she reached for her teeth. She called my name out with a shriek. I went running.

"What did you put in the water to soak my teeth in? They've dissolved!"

I looked. Her teeth were in her mouth; she had forgotten

to put them in the cleanser. We laughed long and often about the time I "dissolved" her teeth.

My mother is now with the Lord. I can imagine her saying to Jesus, "Wait till I tell You this one!"

There are days when life seems to be too serious and I long for my mother's sense of humor to tickle my funny bone. At times the Lord lets me see His sense of humor and I especially appreciate that. He tells me there is a time to laugh and that eternity will be filled with joy.

Father, thank You for the gift of laughter, the joy of memory, and for the promise of things to come.

—**Diane Mitchell**

BREAKING

DOWN BARRIERS

Bear with each other and forgive whatever grievances
you may have against one another.
Forgive as the Lord forgave you.
— Colossians 3:13 NIV

I was sitting at my computer one day, editing what I had written in my book manuscript, *T*L*C for Aging Parents*. The words on the screen said: "We honor our parents because we have received so much from them, including life itself. Our gratitude often is mixed with resentment about their perceived shortcomings and imperfections. Honoring our parents has nothing to do with whether or not we like them. It means, rather, not shaming them verbally or minimizing the investment they have made in our lives."

The interaction of daily caregiving with my mother had caused little irritants which rose to volcanic intensity. I had already gone through the biblical process of releasing hurts and allowing God to heal.

On this particular day, I felt impressed God was saying, "You cannot go on writing this book until you take care of one more thing. Make a list of *your* offenses toward your mother."

I pulled a sheet of paper from my desk drawer, picked up a pen, and listed *my* wrongs in relationship to mother: impatience, insensitivity, intolerance, ungratefulness, and slander. (I had often shared her faults with others.)

I bowed my head and prayed, "God, forgive me." Then I went to my mother's bedside, picked up her bony hand, and said, "Mother, I have not always been patient with you. Please forgive me."

I knew I had shared her faults with my brothers and others. I sat down and wrote letters which said, "I was wrong. Please forgive me." What a sense of release, freedom, and joy I began experiencing in my life.

For the first time in forty-seven years, I felt love for my mother, and I was able to express it. If she was sitting in her wheelchair watching TV, I would extend my arms around her shoulders, give her a squeeze, and say, "I love you." I would pat her arm lovingly every time I fed her.

Each night before turning out the light, I opened her worn King James Bible and read. Then I would pray. Sometimes I thanked God for giving me such a multi-talented, creative mother who carried intense burdens for the spiritual welfare of others. On other occasions I thanked Him for giving me a mother who faithfully taught Sunday school and showed me through example the importance of reaching children.

Then I would lean over, kiss her on the forehead, and say, "I love you." These three little words I had easily spoken all my life to my daddy. Before now, they had always been hard to say to Mother. Now I meant them, and felt them, deep within. The barrier was down.

Father, help me to forgive as You forgave me. Help me to daily love as You love.

—Betty Benson Robertson

I'LL SEE YOU
TOMORROW

*Now glory be to God who by his mighty power at work
within us is able to do far more than we would ever
dare to ask or even dream of.*
—Ephesians 3:20 TLB

Pick up the green crayon and color the grass," I spoke softly. Slowly Dad's eyes moved back and forth carefully scanning the row of crayons lined up on the table. Hesitantly, he chose the brown one. "Take another look," I said gently. He seemed perplexed, so I gave him the green one.

How hard it was for me to watch as Dad jaggedly colored in the grass and then had trouble locating the next crayon. A vibrant man only a few weeks before, a stroke now left him physically weak and disoriented. His speech was also slow, and he had trouble remembering names and events.

It was a big step for me bringing Dad home to live with us, one at first I was reluctant to take. I had heard such negative feedback from people who had parents living with them, that I almost decided against it. I wasn't sure I could handle the responsibility of taking care of him, my husband, and our boys. But I stepped out in faith, and, as always, God's grace was consistently more than sufficient.

Dad's recovery was a slow process. At first, a registered therapist came to our home, but Dad soon dismissed her. He preferred my help. Following her instructions, I made a card for each day of the week and for each month to help him remember. I purchased a grade school number book to reteach him addition and subtraction. Day after day, we sat together at my dining room table, and little by little our perseverance paid off.

What started out as a difficult task turned out to be a very special time for me. As a child I never saw Dad a lot. He worked long hours and was too tired to play with me when he was at home. Even after I married, I didn't see Dad often as I was busy raising our five sons. But now, fifty-two years later, God made up for those lost moments by blessing the two of us with many precious hours together.

As he grew stronger, we went on short shopping trips and out to lunch. Each night while we watched TV together, we held hands—something we had never done before. Dad didn't know how to show affection, nor could he say "I love you," but being with him each day I felt his love in many other ways.

Our special time together lasted only six months. Our last visit was in the hospital, the day before Dad died. As I left his room, he called out to me, "I'll see you tomorrow." But during the night, he died peacefully in his sleep.

Though I never got to speak to Dad again, I am com-

forted by God's promise that I will see him "tomorrow"—
for in God's eyes "a thousand years are like a day" (2 Pet.
3:8 NIV).

*Lord, I am so grateful that You are never reluctant to
help me. How blessed I am to be Your child.*

—Frances Gregory Pasch

Yesterday and Today

Today
I washed Dad's hands,
took wrinkled fingers
in my own,
washed them with love,
warm water, and soap.
Once
he did the same
for me.

—Cora Scott Howell

IS TODAY
SUNDAY?

And God is able to make all grace abound toward you.
—2 Corinthians 9:8 NKJV

This morning, again, Mom Evans came into the kitchen all spruced up, looking lovely. She was ready for church!

"Is today Sunday?" she asked.

"No, Mom, today is Monday," I answered.

On an average of three days out of seven she will come from her bedroom all dressed up and ask the same question.

Mom Evans put her trust in Jesus Christ as Savior and Lord when she was a young mother. She became a strong Christian, deeply grounded in God's Word, and very active in church. Even to this day, at age eighty-two, she is deeply devoted to Christ and loves to go to church.

During the summer of 1991, it became apparent that Mom was becoming forgetful. The doctor called her condition a form of dementia which would not get any better. By fall of that year, we brought her to live with us.

Sometimes I cry. I lock myself in the bathroom or go for a drive so that no one will see me cry. I do not want my husband to think his mother is too much of a burden, and I certainly do not want Mom to ever get the impression that she has complicated my life. It's just when I find an entire load of dirty dishes put away, or find she has washed a large load of clothes in a small amount of water, or misplaced our letters, books, magazines, or clothes, frustration sometimes overwhelms me.

I do not blame Mom. My problem is with myself. At those times I call on the Lord for His grace and patience to be worked in me. Somehow, mysteriously, He makes me aware of His love, assuring me that He understands my frustrations. He then gives me grace to get through another day.

I know she will continue to come from her bedroom dressed for church and ask, "Is today Sunday?" But every time she does, it will be a beautiful reminder of the kind of life she has lived and is living . . . a life fully dedicated to her Lord.

Dearest Father, please help me to be a comfort and joy to Mom in her old age. Thank You for Your grace. Thank You for Your patience with me!

—Loretta K. Evans

AS SHE ONCE

DRESSED ME

For the perishable must clothe itself with the imperishable.
—1 Corinthians 15:53 NIV

When I was a toddler, my mother dressed me each day, sometimes more than once! She pulled my wriggly arms through the sleeves of an undershirt, carefully slipped the dress over my head, and fastened the little buttons on the back. Then she pulled socks on my feet and buckled my patent leather shoes. Working in the basement, Mom washed the daily quota of soiled clothes in an old wringer washing machine. She didn't complain.

Incredibly, the day came when I had to dress my mother. It started slowly. First, she just needed help in tugging up a back zipper. Then I started tying her shoes. In her confusion, she forgot how to tell back and front, inside and outside. Her fingers fumbled at buttons. Eventually, I was helping her with every article of clothing, carefully lifting her arm through a sleeve, putting on stockings, tying a belt. Each day's soiled laundry was easily washed in an automatic machine, but the dailyness of her care bore down on me.

Since her death, I have rejoiced in the assurance that she is no longer weak and helpless. She is now clothed in the eternal garments provided by God the Father for those who trust in His Son.

Heavenly Father, thank You for clothing us with Your nature. Give us strength for daily caring.

—**Eleanor P. Anderson**

My Mother, My Child

I was your baby, you guided my path,
Heard my first cry, first word, and first laugh.
I've been your little girl for many years,
Your pride and your joy in spite of some tears.
Now you're my "child" at age eighty-seven;
And will be, I guess, 'til you go to heaven.
Our roles now are switched, you're in my care;
A more precious burden I never will bear.
I pray that with God's help I truly can be,
The patient "mother" you've been to me.
"The daughter's the mother," in our case it's true;
But, there's one consolation, my model was you.

—**Elaine Cunningham**

❧
UNACCEPTABLE,

BUT COMFORTED

*You can be sure that the more we undergo sufferings
for Christ, the more he will shower us with
his comfort and encouragement.*
—2 Corinthians 1:5 TLB

The lot of caring for Mother has fallen upon my sisters.
I like to think it's because they are in New York and I'm
in southern Maryland. But, to tell the truth, my mother is
so irritated by my presence she doesn't want me around.
She gets terribly upset when I'm with her for any length of
time.

After searching my heart and praying for God's guidance, I can only say Mother is surely my "irregular person." My sisters have assured me I do nothing to warrant
her hostility toward me.

My responding to Mother's ill-treatment toward me in
a Christlike manner only brings forth more verbal abuse,
not less. Over the years I have thought of many plausible
reasons that may have contributed to this behavior pattern,
but none lessen the phenomenal hurt.

My sister continues to bring Mother to my home for a

short stay at Easter. Mother loves the early spring in this area, especially after the long, cold New York winters. Each time I hope this visit will be one of sheer enjoyment in our togetherness as we celebrate our Lord's resurrection.

Early Easter morn in my fifty-ninth year I bumped into Mother in the dark hallway of my home. We were both creeping quietly to avoid waking anyone not wanting to attend the sunrise service. I immediately apologized, hugged her, and then said, "Happy Easter, Mama. I love you!"

For the first time in my entire life I heard her respond, "And I love you too!" I was so elated I hurried into my oldest daughter's room. Like a small child I bounced on her bed saying over and over, "My mommy said she loved me!"

In the six years since that Easter, I have heard my mother tell me, "I love you" three other times. Has this helped me? Yes, in some ways. But I still ache to be around her without her going into tirades. I ache to comfort her as I was not comforted by her. I ache to share Jesus' love with her and give her the comfort He has given me. I want to spend time in a mother-daughter relationship that would enrich us both. It seems this is not to be and I feel saddened.

The role of the caregiver must be a great burden. I do not mean to minimize that heavy weight, but I also know it is a great burden for me to realize I will never be acceptable in my mother's eyes for that position. I only wish I could share the caregiver's burden.

Father, thank You for making me acceptable to You

through Jesus. May I share Your love, comfort, and encouragement with those in need.

—Mary Fender

From the Good Shepherd

To the sheep with the heavy heart
who wets pillows with your tears:
I have arms to wrap around you;
I have strength and listening ears.

To the sheep with the trembling voice
who wonders which way to go:
I have eyes that see the valleys
where the tattered breezes blow.

To the sheep with the weary soul
whose strength and faith is weak:
I'll bring you to My pastures green
And give you all you seek.

—Sherri Langton

The Prize

I stay inside the house each day
and answer every call.
I fix her everything she wants
and hardly mind at all.

I sit with patience by her side
and hear my mom complain.
I hold her hand throughout the night
when she is racked with pain.

My sister flies in for the day.
Mom tells her she is fine
and sings her virtues on and on
but never mentions mine.

But even through the jealousy
I'm thankful to the Lord,
for giving me the time we've shared,
and that is my reward.

—**Marsha Owens Hood**

꙰

TO PRAY AND

NOT TO FAINT

He shall regard the prayer of the destitute,
And shall not despise their prayer.
—Psalm 102:17 NKJV

This was a trying pregnancy, fraught with physical problems and petty annoyances. More aggravating than my two lively daughters, aged six and three, was the gloomy presence of my father-in-law who had lived with us since the death of his wife two years before. Although not in robust health, Dad had, it seemed to me, stopped trying to cope with living. He sat in his room, not reading any of the magazines we bought for him or trying any of the hobbies we so hopefully suggested.

Why his passiveness bothered me so much I can't say. Perhaps it was the contrast to my own condition, full of life in the truest sense. Perhaps it was my innate selfishness that wanted my husband for myself and my time for the children rather than worrying about preparing meals that would satisfy Dad's ever-changing tastes. Maybe it was because I sensed his psychological withdrawal and feared physical inactivity would have a negative effect on his health. But whatever the reason, I found myself becoming more and more depressed.

My husband had enough concerns about his job and providing for a growing family. He, too, was at a loss as to how to integrate his father into our lives. To spare him further worry and not to alarm my little girls, I began to take solitary walks after dark to cry without being seen or heard.

Fortunately, the Lord hears the cries of the afflicted, and before long my tears turned into pleas for His help. There was no reassuring voice from the heavens, no sudden burst of understanding, yet somehow God gave me strength to keep on going. Tears brought release, but prayer empowered me.

Not all caregiving is physical. It may even be easier to tend a parent's physical needs than it is to deal with their psychological disabilities—or our own. But whatever we are called upon to do, we may be sure that His grace is available through prayer and is sufficient for our needs.

Lord, teach us to pray always and not to despair.

—Flora M. Smith

THE DINNER
PARTY

*"Why are you bothering this woman?
She has done a beautiful thing to me."*
—Matthew 26:10 NIV

You're doing fine," the surgeon said.

"Thank you, Doctor."

"Don't mention it. I had fun."

Fun? The operation left my mother with nine months of excruciating pain, depression, and very little improvement.

I cooked special foods. ["That tastes like sawdust."] I found her favorite flowers. ["Those freesia are such a strange color."] I wore the dress she'd made me. ["Why do you wear that thing so often?"] My sister sent autumn leaves and bittersweet. [Take that stuff out of here. It makes me cough.] Those were the good days!

Then came an occasional fleeting smile when she heard a familiar melody. One day she said thank you to a friend who brought homemade applesauce. Gradually pain subsided; depression lifted; surprises came.

One evening she said, "I think I'll have a party."

"Wonderful," I chirped. "What shall I make?"

"Nothing, dear. It's my party. I'll prepare it."

"But . . ."

"I'll just do a little each day."

Sometimes she managed a half hour, sometimes only fifteen minutes, but eventually she had everything ready in the freezer.

Although Mother insisted on ironing the cutwork table-cloth that her mother had embroidered for her own hope chest, I was allowed to do windows and silver. Her guests would do the serving and clearing; I would do the dishes after work.

When I arrived home, I found Mother in bed. "We had the best time! Everyone relaxed," she said with a smile, "even Mr. Longworth. By the way, would you get me two pills from the top drawer of the vanity?" She was in agony.

"Why didn't you let me do it?" I scolded.

"I had to. One last party. You do understand, don't you?"

Suddenly, cutting through my righteous indignation came the picture of the disciples chiding Mary for "wasting" her expensive perfume. Like Mary's anointing of Jesus, my mother's dinner party was a gesture of love and leave-taking, a gift that cost greatly but was absolutely necessary.

Lord, forgive my bossiness, my trying to force Mother to be "sensible." Help me to stand back and let her use her time and the little energy she has the way she needs to use it.

—Ruth Harrison

My Everything

You are my Savior
You are my Lord.
You feed me with
Your precious Word

You give me joy.
You give me hope.
You are my strength
You help me cope.

You are my life.
In You I rest.
With You as Lord,
I am my best.

—Frances Gregory Pasch

INTERRUPTIONS

For we do not have a high priest
who is unable to sympathize with our weaknesses,
but we have one who has been tempted in every way,
just as we are—yet was without sin.
—Hebrews 4:15 NIV

Exhausted at the end of a stress-filled day, I pulled the bedroom door shut and fell on my knees. I'd prayed for only a few minutes when Mom's cry of anguish pierced the silence. Instantly, I dragged myself to my feet and headed for her hospital bed.

The misery in Mom's eyes and her cries wrenched my heart. I'd already given her pain medicine. I helped her situate herself to the least painful position she could find and tucked the blankets around her shoulders.

"You go on to bed now," she directed. "I'll try not to bother you anymore."

I walked back down the hall and again slipped to my knees. "Excuse me, God, for just taking off," I whispered. "Mom hurts so badly. And I feel so helpless. And tired. And frustrated. I need strength from You." Tears splashed on the bedspread. "But I can't even spend time with You without interruption."

I didn't see a light or hear a voice. But suddenly, words etched themselves in my mind: "Service is a high form of prayer."

I thought about my Savior. When He heard that John the Baptist had been beheaded, Jesus jumped in a boat and headed for a solitary place. He needed to work through the loss, frustration, and pain quietly, privately, with His Father. But someone saw Him leave. They watched the direction He headed. They told their friends. And a crowd hurried to the place they expected Jesus to come ashore.

As Jesus approached the shore, He saw thousands on the hillside waiting for Him. His opportunity for needed solitude had vanished. What feelings flashed through Him in that instant? Disappointment? Exhaustion? Frustration?

Jesus felt fatigue and disappointment. He felt His need for time alone with His Father. "The Son can do nothing of himself," He said (John 5:19 KJV). But He also was "moved with compassion toward them" (Matt. 14:14 KJV). He held tightly to His ongoing friendship with the Father as He ministered to their needs.

Jesus understands my need for solitude, for communion with God. He understands the disappointment of interruptions. He understands that sometimes serving must supersede solitude. And He holds on to me as I hold on to Him.

Thank You, Jesus, that You understand me, that You are moved with compassion toward me, and that You move me with compassion to serve.

—Helen Heavirland

W h e n e v e r

Whenever days are harried,
When nights are dark and long,
I look to God my Father,
He fills my life with song.

Whenever dreams are tumbling,
When all my skies are gray,
I turn my eyes toward heaven,
He always shows the way.

It matters not for what I pray,
How foolish seem my tears.
Whenever I pray   . He answers,
Whenever I cry . . . He hears.

—Marcia Krugh Leaser

GOD OF

ALL COMFORT

I will not leave you comfortless: I will come to you.
—John 14:18 KJV

I reached to help as Mother's trembling fingers attempted to button her blouse. "Wouldn't you be more comfortable in your robe today?" I suggested.

I should have known better. Mother always believed in dressing when she rose in the morning. It was not her habit to sit around in her robe. Tears filled her eyes as she shook her head and spoke softly, "No, I'll feel better if I'm dressed."

I nodded, remembering her tall, erect figure and neat appearance.

"You must go to church this morning," she pleaded. "Dad and I will be all right."

It had been a long time since I had left them alone and I felt uneasy. Besides, I was bone tired. But Mother insisted. It was important to her and the church was nearby, so I dressed in a hurry, knowing I would be late.

Weary in body, distressed in mind, I entered the church. Taking the hymnbook handed to me, I sank into a pew near the back. But I couldn't sing. Clutching the hymnal to my breast, I let the music and the words pour into my heart like the warmth of a healing balm. Every word of the old hymn seemed meant for me.

"Spirit of God, descend upon my heart . . ."*

"Oh, yes, Lord, Your Spirit, Your love, Your strength—descend upon my heart."

As my tears flowed, God the Holy Spirit drew near surrounding me with His loving presence.

Knowing my need, the Comforter calmed my tangled emotions, understood my weariness, spoke peace to my troubled thoughts.

I could return home to care for my parents, knowing that He is not a far-off God. Rather He is a living, all-knowing God who reaches down with compassion to answer the cry of His children.

Dear heavenly Father, thank You for coming with Your comforting presence just when I need You.

—Florence E. Parkes

* "Spirit of God, Descend Upon My Heart," George Croly, 1780 –1860.

CHOOSING
TO LOVE

*Love is very patient and kind. . . . If you love someone
you will be loyal to him no matter what the cost.*
—1 Corinthians 13:4, 7 TLB

Mother was more confused than usual this morning.
She insisted on wearing shoes that didn't match. She
couldn't find the bathroom. And she got in and out of her
coat half a dozen times although I kept telling her we
weren't going anywhere. Finally, in desperation, I decided
to take her shopping. *Maybe,* I told myself, *a ride in the
car will do her good.*

And it did! The motion of the car had the same soothing
effect on my mother that it had on my babies. By the time
we got to the store she was quiet and relaxed.

"Do you mind waiting in the car while I run in for just
a minute?" I asked her.

She yawned and nodded her head.

I parked where I could keep an eye on her and flipped
on the safety locks. I knew she didn't know how to unlock
the car. For that matter, it had been over a year since she'd
been able to figure out how to unfasten her seat belt.

When I got back to the car, I was greeted by a flat tire. "This is just what I need," I moaned.

"Can I help you?" Mom asked.

"No, Mom. Just be quiet. Okay?"

The tire wasn't all the way flat, so I decided to risk driving to a nearby gas station. I took the fastest way out of the shopping plaza, ignoring the in and out arrows. I knew I was wrong, but I was careful. I left plenty of room for the approaching car to go around me. But instead of moving to the side, the driver slammed on his brakes and shouted obscenities at me.

My flat tire forgotten, I went into a tirade about the way some men treat women and children. How dare he call me such a filthy name!

In the midst of my loud and angry reaction, Mom reached over and patted my arm. "I love you, dear," she said softly.

My anger drained from me. Seeing me at my worst, my mother chose to love me and to show her love. Had I given her the same gift?

Lord, thank You for the gift of a mother who chooses to love me even when I'm not at my best. Help me to give her the same gift.

—Marlene Bagnull

I MUST

BE CRAZY

For I know the plans I have for you, says the Lord.
They are plans for good and not for evil,
to give you a future and a hope.
—Jeremiah 29:11 TLB

I have a daughter named Lyn, but she never comes to see me anymore. I don't think I even know where she is." Mom sounded sad and bewildered.

"Mom, I'm Lyn. I'm your daughter. I'm right here with you." The words burst out of me.

She stared at me, disbelief warring with fright.

My sister shook her head in warning: Don't do this to her.

I couldn't stop myself. I couldn't bear that Mom thought I had abandoned her.

"Mom, please believe what I'm telling you. I'm your daughter."

Mom struggled out of her chair and stumbled from the room. We could hear her sobbing in the bedroom.

"Let her be," my sister cautioned. "She'll forget all about this in a little while."

179

But I couldn't heed her words. Tears streaming down my face, I hurried to Mom. She was huddled on the bed, her thin body heaving with her sobs.

I put my arms around her and she nestled close. We sat together for a long time, our shared grief bringing a measure of comfort.

"I must be c-c-crazy," Mom finally stammered through her tears. "H-how could I not know my own daughter!"

I hugged her to me. "You're not crazy, Mom. Sometimes you have problems with your memory, that's all. Don't worry about it. We'll just remind you when you forget."

We both knew it wasn't that simple.

As the months pass, Mom knows me less and less of the time. I no longer attempt to jog her memory. I no longer try to convince her that her "Lyn" hasn't abandoned her.

I have agonized in prayer over the loss of my mother in this terrible way that often seems worse than death. Gently, tenderly, the Lord has brought me to the understanding that I must release that person my mother used to be. I must let go of all my expectations of her and accept the reality of who she is today. I must give my mother to the Lord and acknowledge His sovereign right to be in control over her life. My role is simply to trust with absolute faith in His loving plan.

Sovereign God, You have given me the assurance that Your plans for each of us are for good and not evil. Help me to rest in that promise and trust in Your perfect wisdom.
—Lyn Jackson

C o n t r o l

When reality batters and breaks me,
my hope hugs the sidelines,
my faith loses pace;
when discouragement shatters and shakes me
and tempts me to quit,
to concede in the race—
I hold to this truth for trusting;
it fastens my eyes on the goal.
I've measured its length
and tested its strength:
God is in control.

—Sherri Langton

✍

THE SILVER

BUTTER DISH

Let us not become weary in doing good, for at the
proper time we will reap a harvest if we do not give up.
—Galatians 6:9 NIV

How I hated those doilies! After my mother-in-law moved in with us, scraps of crochet work spread over my furniture like a fungus. Her Victorian armchairs elbowed aside my Danish modern ones.

I wanted her to feel at home, but Jenny acted as if the house were hers. She sometimes treated me as if I were a guest who had outstayed my welcome.

At first, I thought this was a method of tormenting me. Gradually, I began to realize that Jenny wasn't "all there" mentally. I prayed for patience.

Jenny treasured her possessions. Those she valued most she locked up in a big, fragrant chest that she kept in her bedroom. When small items began to disappear, I suspected my children or their friends. One day, my sterling silver butter dish was missing. A thrill of alarm crawled up my spine.

The kids wouldn't have taken that. Was it a burglar?

Some time after that, I was helping Jenny clean her room. I gasped when she opened her cedar chest. There were my missing knickknacks.

Jenny snatched my hand away as I reached in. "Don't bother with my things."

"Do something," I stormed at my husband. "She's even got my can opener in there."

He shrugged helplessly. "I guess you'll just have to keep your stuff locked up."

Jenny's health slowly deteriorated. She began to be bedridden, off and on. This put an unbearable squeeze on my time. At the end of each day, I was exhausted and irritable.

I was so busy, I forgot to draw on my spiritual resources. I skipped church more often than not. I would listen to my children's prayers, then forget to say my own. But even though I neglected the Lord, He stayed faithful to me.

There were times when, wrestling with basins and bedpans, I would hate the sight of Jenny's wasted body. It was then that the Lord would whisper gently, "You're doing it for Me."

Shortly before she died, Jenny presented me with a clumsily wrapped gift.

"This is one of my nicest things," she said. "I wanted you to have it because you've been so good to me."

I treasured that moment and the gift—even though it turned out to be my own silver butter dish.

Father God, please lend us Your patience when ours is in short supply. During the weary times, help us to lean back in Your loving arms.

—Beverly Eliason

I Don't Understand

Lord, I don't understand
how Your Spirit
can dwell within me.
I don't understand
how He can change me.
But I do understand
why I need
all You have for me.
Thank You for meeting me
at my point of weakness,
for filling me with power
to be all You call me to be.
Thank You, Lord,
for Your Holy Spirit.

—Marlene Bagnull

THE NURSING HOME
DECISION

If any of you lacks wisdom,
he should ask God,
who gives generously to all
without finding fault,
and it will be given to him.

James 1:5 NIV

Wisdom! How I needed it as Mom's condition worsened and her care required more and more of me. I knew the day was coming when we might not be able to continue to care for her in our home, and yet I had promised myself I would *not* put her in a nursing home. If ever I felt I was in a no-win situation, it was now. If I put Mom in a nursing home, I would be failing her. And yet, as friends pointed out, if I didn't, I would be failing my husband and children. "They need to come first," more than one person told me.

"But Mom has no one but us," I argued. "I can't abandon her to strangers in a nursing home who may or may not take good care of her."

Putting Mom in a nursing home was the most difficult and painful decision I ever had to make. I still remember packing her suitcase, walking her to the car, the look in her eyes when she realized I was leaving her . . .

How can you find the wisdom God promises to give, and His peace, as you grapple with the nursing home decision?

Listen to the counsel of others. It was easier to tune out what my friends were saying than to listen. But when the doctor who cared for me and my mother told me it was time—told me I could no longer give Mom the care she needed—I listened. That same evening, the Christian counselor I had been seeing once or twice a month repeated, almost exactly, my doctor's words. Both of them knew me well. Both had promised they would support my decision to care for Mom in my home as long as it was the best thing for all of us.

With an objectivity I did not have, they both saw what I had been refusing to see. Not only did Mom need care we could not give her, my husband and children needed me. The price tag they were paying was too high. I could not sacrifice the living to care for the dying.

Trust God to go before you and prepare a place for your parent. Visit nursing homes with your eyes wide open and your list of questions prepared. The books recommended in the bibliography on page 375 will help you to know what to look for and what to ask. But expect God's confirmation in special and surprising ways and through the peace He will give you.

Rely on God's strength for the days ahead. Releasing your loved one to the care of others will change, but not diminish, your special role as caregiver. Your parent still needs you but in different ways. Do not allow yourself to feel like a failure. You've done what is best for your parent, for the rest of your family, and for yourself.

GOD'S

MIRACLES

*For they had not understood about the loaves, because
their heart was hardened.*
—Mark 6:52 NKJV

When Dad had a second stroke after a long period of deteriorating health, I knew I'd have to admit that I could no longer care for him at home. After he'd been hospitalized for several days, a friend asked, "When do you think he'll get home?" I guess my reply that he wouldn't be coming home must have sounded pretty hopeless to her.

"Oh, you can't know that," she protested. "There could be a miracle. We can pray for him."

"Yes, there are miracles," I replied. "But I think we've had a large share of miracles already, and God's miracles usually seem to make sense." It just didn't seem to make sense to ask for a miraculous reversal of the normal aging process in a man ninety years old.

When I took time to list all the miracles we had already experienced, I was amazed. Finding caregivers who had just the right skills and personal characteristics to fit our needs, including one who gained new skills as our needs

189

changed. Dry weather while we built a downstairs bedroom and bath for Dad, but rain just after I leveled and reseeded the lawn.

There was a miraculous answer to prayer on an icy winter night when Dad's agitation indicated the possibility that he had suffered another stroke. I asked God to let me avoid taking him to the hospital on icy roads, and Dad soon fell asleep.

And then there was a message so clear it might actually have been spoken, "You see, I am taking care of everything. Don't worry. It will be okay." This came after Dad had become so extremely agitated that he definitely had to be hospitalized. It was an incredibly warm, sunny, February day. My sister and I were both home with him because of an unexpected school board decision to change the school calendar making that day a winter holiday.

If I will gain by enduring instead of escaping, I pray that God will not allow my heart to be too hard to recognize the miracle of His presence, His care, and His love even in the midst of turmoil.

Dear Lord, I know You are able to heal and deliver in spectacular ways, but today I thank You for opening my eyes to Your continual everyday care.

—Helen Kammerdiener

SEEKING

PEACE

So I decided to take Wisdom home to live with me,
because I knew that she would give me good advice and
encourage me in times of trouble and grief.
—Wisdom 8:9 TEV

It was hard to see the mother who had taught me how to
dress, cook, and set a pretty table forgetting all her good
manners. By ninety she was paranoid, hostile to helpers,
and denying her loneliness and growing confusion with the
faucets, stove, and calendar. An overnight companion and
meals-on-wheels were too frail a support system. Yet
Mother insisted with childlike hubris, "I'm going to stay
in my own house." She referred to me as "bossy."

"Mother needs full-time care," I told my sibs, only to
meet with anger and denial. Our conflict was one of the
saddest things about Mother's decline. I, nearest at two
hundred miles away, was most in touch with Mom's subtle
changes. The other three, slower to accept the truth, saw
me as cruel to notice her shortcomings, choosing to believe
her words on the phone that she was happy and competent.

Our stages of grief, I now see, were not coinciding.

While I, the independent youngest, was realistically sizing up nursing homes, my siblings found standing up to their feisty but failing parent unthinkable. Fervently, I prayed we four unique individuals would survive the unhappy situation with love intact.

Mother's last December in her own home, which I helped her celebrate, was a painful but growing time for me. "God," I said one afternoon, flinging myself to my knees, "I give up having to know everything, having to be right, having to have control." It brought me a welcome sense of peace, and shortly I gained fresh insight. While sometimes we may be wrong, at other times, acting on inner wisdom and compassion and professional guidance, we may be wise to take some control in a deteriorating situation. If it means braving the scorn of relatives, the main thing is helping the hurting one—not proving who is right or wrong.

Eventually, a majority of us agreed on Mother's need for placement, but we couldn't decide where. Deciding which sister would get the responsibility and honor of having her near was touchy. Mother's fondness for New England helped us settle on a well-run facility near me which offered a room with a view.

Together we sisters prepared for our mother's entry into the gracious home. There, proximity to gentle hills and caring family brought her comfort as she gradually retreated far into the past, dying fourteen months later. Unacknowledged family tensions, however, strove to undo us as we divided the contents of her house. But love fought back. Focusing on family unity and choosing to forgive, in time we saw the results for which I had sought prayer. Today we demonstrate our unbroken ties, celebrating a legacy of love Mother would surely have wanted us to share.

Lord Jesus, help us to focus on our ultimate goal, harmony. Enable us through the difficult times, by Your presence and example, to grow more loving.

—**Phoebe Bell Honig**

FOR GOD ALL

THINGS ARE POSSIBLE

But Jesus looked at them and said to them, "With men this is impossible, but with God all things are possible."
—Matthew 19:26 NKJV

A *nursing home.* I heard the words, but I could not believe them. A nursing home was only for aged people who didn't have any relatives to care for them, wasn't it? Certainly, it was not an option for my own father. Yet as the social worker explained the situation to my mother and me, we realized that she was right. After six months of hospitalization for Parkinson's disease, my father was still too weak to go home. A nursing home seemed our only recourse.

But who would tell my father that he was to be put in a nursing home? After nearly a half year of looking forward to his hospital release, who would tell him that he could not come back home?

My heart sank as the social worker at the hospital questioned my mother about her finances. My parents had worked hard all of their lives, but it would be impossible for them to afford the care that my father now so desperately needed.

I miss being home. My father's words echoed in my mind. Each time I visited him he was eager for news about home. From his hospital bed, he still reminded my mother about getting a new furnace filter, where to spray for ants, and where to purchase a hose replacement. Thoughts of getting back to his own house and garden had helped to buoy my father's spirits during his long hospital stay. *Now, I asked myself, would his health worsen when he heard the news?*

"We'll have to phone all of those nursing homes and visit them too," my mother was telling me. Her voice brought me back to reality. We had to make plans now. It was our responsibility not only to choose a good nursing home, but somehow to find the financial means to pay for it.

That evening, as I sat down for my daily devotions, I prayed for God's guidance in the weeks ahead. I was reminded of His promise that "with God all things are possible" (Matt. 19:26 NKJV).

"Lord, You know what my parents and I are facing," I prayed. "Our situation seems to overwhelm us. But You have assured us that it is not impossible if we leave it with You. Please take our needs, Father, and work things out for Your glory."

I closed my Bible and got up from the table. No matter what the future held for our family, I knew that God was watching over us. The situation we faced was extremely difficult—but it was not impossible.

Lord, help us to place our problems in Your hands. We know that with You all things are possible.

—**Carolyn Bolz**

Today Is Not Forever

Today is not forever—
   Its trials soon will be
A part of time forgotten
   When end results I see.
Today is not forever—
   God's grace will make a way;
Not now for all tomorrow,
   But all I need today.

—**Merna B. Shank**

SECRETS

OF LOVE

"For there is nothing hidden which will not be revealed, nor has anything been kept secret but that it should come to light."
—Mark 4:22 NKJV

Evacuating a pesky raccoon from her attic was frustrating for my eighty-year-old mother, but she overcame the frightful experience just the way she overcomes other difficulties.

The huge glaring eyes still haunted her. The crushed Christmas ornaments, shredded wrapping paper, and scattered traces of once treasured trinkets she cleaned up symbolized many other hurdles she had conquered. Although one of her sons offered to help, she insisted on doing it herself.

The memories of the uninvited visitor softened when Mom unfolded a dusty local history paper that I wrote in grade school. She phoned shortly after sorting through the attic debris, jubilant about the treasure that the furry critter had so uniquely uncovered. Later, her heart swelled when she learned that the raccoon had been making a nest. She recalled nesting the seven of us in her heart.

Mom broke her hip a month ago and wanted to go home shortly after surgery. "When can I drive? In a couple of weeks?" she asked.

It was difficult to tell her that she couldn't go home until she regained her strength. She said that we were hurting her and didn't love her enough.

As I gathered Mom's clothes for her stay in an assisted-living apartment, I found some letters tucked in a corner of her chest of drawers. They were over thirty-five years old; ones I sent while away at school.

The fact that she saved my letters tells me that she still believes in my love. I hope she knows that the love I sent in letters many years ago is still unfolding.

Thank You, Father, for revealing what was hidden so love and understanding can come to light.

—**Carol Stevens Leonard**

NOT

GUILTY

Commit to the LORD whatever you do,
and your plans will succeed.
—Proverbs 16:3 NIV

I can't seem to rid myself of this guilty feeling," my friend said as we sipped our coffee.

How well I identified with her pain and frustration at placing her parent in a nursing home. I had experienced the same thing last year. I felt I was giving my responsibility to someone else, even to strangers who could not possibly love my parent as I did. I still needed to be in control. After all, how could a nursing home provide the intimate care that my parent deserved? Wouldn't I be neglecting one who had done so much for me? Wouldn't I be failing to fulfill one of the things God might be expecting me to do?

After I grappled with these and many other emotional questions that absorbed my thinking, intelligence with God's help began to take charge. And intelligent decision-making is what He really expects!

Could I continue to assist my parent to a chair in a professional way which would not physically hurt him and which was becoming more necessary each day? What if he accidentally fell because of my inability to support his weight? My home did not possess IVs and other medical provisions that might suddenly be demanded for his immediate care.

Yes, my friend's guilty feelings were once mine. They did not immediately pass after my parent became a nursing home resident. But with time, God's comfort and assurance became evident.

After visiting with my parent the other day, I smiled as I left him with other residents who were waiting for him to begin their daily domino game.

Dear heavenly Father, help me to constantly seek Your guidance, and to be ever mindful of the guidance You give.
—**Mary Beth Nelson**

THROUGH

MOTHER'S EYES

My God will meet all your needs.
—Philippians 4:19 NIV

When my husband's mother needed greater care than we could give her in our home, we had to take her to a nursing home. But I was worried. Alice always had been strong, independent, and feisty. She'd been an active ranch woman with her gardening, canning, and cooking. I was convinced she'd be miserable and feel fenced in.

To my surprise, Alice settled into her room as though it were a cocoon of comfort. Slowly we began to realize that she no longer looked at life as she used to—and as we did.

I worried that time might seem long to her in her new setting, but I was wrong. One day she complained to me, "The days are too short here. Time you dress and have your breakfast, you hardly have time to take a walk down the hall before lunch. Then, after you rest, you hardly have time to visit a bit before it's time for supper and bed!" And I thought that her time would drag!

Then there was the day when a nurse told us they had

to tie her when she sat in her rocker because she couldn't remember that she needed help to stand. Tie up Alice! Unthinkable! But when I walked into her room and saw her in her rocker she said, "Look. See what they did for me so I won't forget and stand up and fall. Isn't this nice of them?" And I thought she would protest loudly that her freedom had been violated!

I remembered hearing Corrie ten Boom tell what her father said to her when, as a little girl, she worried that she would not have the courage to die for Jesus if she had to.

"Corrie, when do I give you the ticket when you take the train to Amsterdam?" he asked her.

"When I get on the train," she answered.

"That's what God does," her father replied. "He gives you the ticket in life just when you need it."

That's what God had done for Alice. He had given her a "ticket" when she needed it and helped her to see life through new eyes. We were all comforted!

Dear Father, thank You that You understand all our needs and meet them so abundantly.

—**Venus E. Bardanouve**

HIS
GIFTS

Whatever you do, work at it with all your heart, as working for the Lord, not for men.
—Colossians 3:23 NIV

After Mother suffered yet another stroke, my brother, husband, and I arranged a family meeting to confront her with the news that she could no longer live alone. But she turned the tables on us. Retaining her dignity and the control of her life, Mother said, "The way I've been falling lately, I think I should go into a nursing home for awhile —just until I get well. What do you think?"

The nursing home had a tastefully appointed reception area with a baby grand piano. Music had been Mother's entire life since age nine when she began playing the pump organ for church services.

Mother ate her meals in the family style dining room after which the residents retreated to the reception area. Mother entertained them by playing the piano. Her repertoire seemed endless—at first.

One day Mother said, "Would you bring me some of my sheet music?"

The next day I brought the music and, with great anticipation, opened to a favorite melody. Mother positioned herself to play, looked up at the music—and gasped. She shook her head as if to clear out the cobwebs or to deny the unthinkable. Then she slammed the book shut and said, "No."

It was clear she could not read the music, but she could not admit it. Instead she responded to the lingering strains of music still active in her fading memory. Christmas was approaching. To the delight of the residents, she played carols.

Christmas came and went. In mid-January, one of the residents said, "Mrs. Hoke, you know Christmas is over."

"Oh, I know it is," Mother replied, "but it's coming again!" Undaunted, she continued playing the only thing she could. She might have continued playing carols into the next Christmas season, but a necessary move to another nursing home (without a baby grand) ended her seventy-five-year love affair with the piano. But she took her adaptability and sense of humor to her new home. Even at that stage of life, she was still teaching us to use our gifts in whatever way we could.

Father God, thank You for the gifts You have given us. May we always put them to good use.

—**Gwen Northcutt**

LEARNED

CONTENTMENT

I have learned in whatever state I am, to be content.
—Philippians 4:11 NKJV

On that Monday morning I could hear my mother whistling when I opened the door to her tiny apartment. It was the same tuneless little tune that meant all was well and she was feeling fine.

"I'm so glad you could come right over," she said, with a hint of excitement in her voice. Then she, who recently had been declared legally blind, led *me* to a chair!

"Sit here," she said. "I have news! They have accepted me at the health care center as a permanent resident! But I must check in on Wednesday morning because there are others waiting."

No, I cried inwardly. *No, no!* Aloud I said, "So soon? I thought there might be a long wait . . ."

We had known for some time that there was no cure for our mother's failing eyesight. Her other health problems were beginning to require more care each day, but living only a few blocks from her apartment it was no task for us to carry in her noon or evening meals and to have her come for overnight visits while allowing her the independence of living in her own home.

I hoped she wouldn't notice the tears that came, but Mother reached for my hand. "I know so many who live at the health care center, it will be a much better situation for me, plus round-the-clock nursing care if I should need it!"

Suddenly I could see my mother's independent spirit coming through again, and I realized she was not just comforting me. Her reasons for going to live at the health care center were valid and wise.

Now more than a year has passed. I often travel the seven miles to visit. I come away amazed at my mother's foresight. I am amazed, too, at the way our heavenly Father smooths our paths as we seek His will and as we learn to be content with the way He chooses for us. For, you see, I had to learn to be content too—content with allowing "strangers" to care for my mother, when I thought only I could, or should, assume her daily care.

Our Father, thank You for Your presence with us wherever we are, and for Your wonderful care every day of our lives.

—Bettie MacMorran

BREAKING
A PROMISE

For I the LORD thy God will hold thy right hand,
saying unto thee, Fear not; I will help thee.
—Isaiah 41:13 KJV

Fear ate at me as I struggled to care for my ill husband and eighty-six-year-old mother who was confused from a stroke. Mom refused to live with us, and her house was a thirty-minute drive through heavy traffic and the highest crime area of our city. Frantic calls from her concerned friends and neighbors often came in the middle of the night. After my last dash through the night, the doctor demanded I place Mom in a nursing home for her own sake. But long ago Mom had made me promise never to put her in a nursing home under any circumstances. I now knew that was a foolish promise for me to make, and I knew I would have to break it.

On the way home, I was too upset to pray anything except, "God, please help me."

My husband was worried, knowing that being caretaker for him and Mom was draining me physically and emotionally. We prayed together.

During the night, I dreamed about Dorothy, Mom's friend who lived in a nursing home. I could hear Mom's words after visiting Dorothy one time. "If I ever *had* to go in a home, that would be the only one."

I called the home early the next morning. Dorothy was still there, and the home did have an opening—in the room with Dorothy. Within a few hours, I'd checked out the home and picked up Mom. How I dreaded her anger when she realized I was leaving her there.

Mom and Dorothy hugged and giggled like happy children. Hand in hand, they went over to the sofa. Mom turned to me. "You run along now. We want to visit."

"She'll be fine," the nurse said.

I stumbled down the walk, blinded by tears. My prayers had been answered beyond my wildest hopes. And the outburst I'd feared from my broken promise never happened. Mom was happy visiting with her friend from church.

Lord, I praise and thank You for holding my hand through the dark shadows of fear.

—Marie Butler

TRUSTING IS BETTER
THAN WORRYING

Thou wilt keep him in perfect peace, whose mind is stayed on thee: because he trusteth in thee.
—Isaiah 26:3 KJV

Placing a parent in a personal care facility is a depressing experience.

My eighty-two-year-old father, who'd lived alone for twelve years, went blind this past Christmas. He begged me to find him a place where he could receive proper care.

Trying to find a suitable facility was a worrisome ordeal. I felt guilty for not taking him into our own home, but I'm a pastor. My wife and I are often not at home, and—well, "home alone" is not a good place to be these days.

After much searching and praying and worrying, we found a place in the Laurel Highlands of western Pennsylvania. I hoped Dad would be comfortable there. He wasn't. His roommate, ninety-four-year-old Jim, wasn't much company. My father wanted to talk about railroading and politics and classical music. All Jim wanted to do was chew and spit.

In our weekly visits, I began to notice how depressed my father was becoming. He paced the hallways with his white cane looking for someone to talk with and not understanding that most of the people who leaned against the hallways were more depressed than he.

Finally I asked the head nurse if she couldn't find him a more talkative roommate. I was overjoyed when she told me she'd move him in with Louie—a cheerful man down the hall who seemed to be a friend to everybody.

About a week later, the nurse told me that Dad refused to be moved. Baffled, I called him to see what had happened.

"Well, you know," he said, "I've decided I kind of like old Jim. In fact, we had a good talk last night. He told me all about his thirty-eight years in the coal mine, and I told him all about my years in the steel mill. And when I told him I might be moving to another room, it sounded like he was about to cry. 'Oh, don't move, Bob,' he said. 'I *love* you!' You know," my father continued, "I think I kinda like the old guy. I told the nurse I'll stay right here."

Since that time, I've noticed a slow but steady improvement in Dad. All he needed was a little time to find a friend, and all I needed was a little time to quit worrying and start trusting again.

Father, forgive me for being such a worrywart. Help me to remember that You love Dad far more than I do and that I will never be mistaken in entrusting him to Your care.
—**Bob Randall**

Touch Me

Her eyes gaze blue,
her cheekbones high and handsome,
their wrinkles peach crinkled satin.
White wisps escape thin smoothing hands,
for trembling fingers miss the pins.
Her proud glance grasps dignity
age and illness steal away.
Sharp-toned she commands,
"Take this away. Bring that to me."
She never knows those blue eyes
plead her soul cry—
"Touch me."

—Cora Scott Howell

TOUGH
DECISIONS

We were pressed out of measure, above strength, . . .
that we should not trust in ourselves, but in God.
—2 Corinthians 1:8–9 KJV

Ruth, you must put your mother in a nursing home," my uncle declared. "Can't you see what you are doing to yourself?"

I ignored him. After all, hadn't my husband and I felt God calling us home from our work as missionaries in Pakistan to care for Mother?

Mom lived in her own apartment and needed a lot of supervision. Parkinson's caused shaking hands and dancing feet. She could no longer feed herself or walk without assistance. Rolling her wheelchair to the curb and lifting her into the car for a doctor's visit exhausted my energy. Meanwhile, I also needed to care for my husband who was recovering from a heart attack.

"Ruth, you must put your mother in the nursing home for a month and get some rest," the doctor insisted when I consulted him because of my high blood pressure.

Mom became distraught at the idea. "I'll not go there!"

she said. And she meant just that! But despite Mom's strong will, daily her body became weaker. She could no longer change from sitting or lying until I came from my apartment. We hired daytime help and slept in her apartment, but often she wanted up six times during the night.

When I talked about admitting her to the nursing home, my husband objected. "We came home so you could care for your mother," he reminded me. "We have to do it."

It would have been impossible for me to follow the advice of my uncle and my doctor when it was contrary to my husband's and mother's wishes had I not experienced very severe chest pains one Sunday night.

I felt the Lord saying, "This is the way. Walk ye in it."

After her admission, Mom's hallucinations were horrible. The staff needed my assistance for ten hours one day. Wildly she glared at me and asked, "Why have you left the corral gate open so the mules can trample over me? Why don't you do something? Get the police after those thieves. They stole everything!"

Today Mom has forgotten those days. Now she says, "I'm glad to be here. The girls take good care of me. Everybody should come here when they can't care for themselves."

Twice a month I have old-time spelling matches with the residents. My ninety-three-year-old blind mother is one of the best spellers. One of the residents says, "Thanks, Ruth, that was fun!"

"I think so too!" my mother echoes.

Thank You, Father, for the comfort You give in Your special ways.

—Ruth E. Montgomery

My Gethsemane

When life is pain
an open sore
and I
in weakness cry
"No more!"
Help me, Father,
pray as He,
"Not my will,
but Thine
for me."

—Marcia Krugh Leaser

THE "CHRISTIAN"
THING TO DO

And the peace of God, which passeth all understanding,
shall keep your hearts and minds.
—Philippians 4:7 KJV

T he nurse from Station Two at the convalescent hospital called on a Monday evening.

"Your grandmother is acting strangely," she said. "She told us that she is 'going home.' I have the feeling if you want to see her alive, you'd best come now."

We found Grandma semiconscious, as if already in the presence of the Lord she had loved for ninety-one of her one hundred and three years. She scarcely responded to our attempts at conversation, and only two statements came from her lips unbidden. One a fragment of Scripture: "The peace of God that passeth all understanding." The other a line from a song she'd sung for as long as I could remember: "The love of God is greater far than tongue or pen can ever tell." *

For the next two weeks, while Grandma hovered between life on earth and life in heaven, a parade of visitors flocked around her bed. Staff members ate their lunches at

215

her bedside. Fellow residents dropped by with grave concern written across their furrowed faces. "How's Blanche today?" they asked, then shook their heads and went away.

Her demented roommate ceased ranting and screaming, as if hushed in memory of the long hours Grandma had spent holding her hand or reading the Bible to her.

Already her friends missed her kind words, her comforting gestures, her clear high soprano voice that filled the halls with praises of her beloved Lord.

At Grandma's memorial service, her admirers sang "How Great Thou Art," the song with which she had blessed them all.

"She was one of God's earth angels," one woman told us.

"She changed my life," said another.

The wife of the lay pastor who led the service summarized it well: "Blanche lived the things my husband preaches."

We smiled and remembered back to the day we'd brought her here. Our hearts had condemned us for not keeping her at home, the "Christian" thing to do. The logic of circumstances and miraculous provision told us it was the only thing to do. Yet on the day we arrived, everything seemed to go wrong. We left Grandma in tears, wailing, "How could you do this to me?"

The director of nursing had looked at us with overflowing empathy and said: "Believe me, you *will* know you have done the right thing—soon."

She was more right than she knew. Within months, Grandma had adjusted to her new assignment. "Of course

I miss my home and family," she told us. "But God has put me here for a reason."

Today we went home from her memorial service knowing that nothing we had ever done for Grandma was so "Christian" as bringing her here to this her final sacred place of ministry.

Dear Father, give me the courage each day to trust You when the caregiver's path You spread before me is obscured with fog, and not demand the sunshine of too-soon answers.

—**Ethel Herr**

❧

WATCHING, WAITING,

AND PRAYING

Give your burdens to the Lord.
He will carry them.

Psalm 55:22 TLB

Recently I got a long overdue and needed haircut. I hadn't realized how much more gray hair I had until the beautician started trimming. My daughter was quick to point out the stripe that looked like a skunk's. Gratefully the trim minimized my "skunk stripe" and gave me more of a salt and pepper look.

"Vanity of vanities," said Solomon. "All is vanity" (Eccl. 12:8 NKJV). But it's more than vanity that has us counting gray hairs. Rare is the man or woman who does not fear the aging process, especially when they see it happening to their mother or father.

Just as we cannot stop gray hairs from growing, there's nothing we can do to stop our once healthy and mentally sharp parent from going downhill. All we really can do is watch, wait, and pray. Sometimes we may feel we can't even do that. Visiting them in the nursing home or hospital may be more than we can emotionally handle. Our visits may become farther and farther apart—not because we don't care, but because we care so much. Others may feel compelled to spend almost every waking moment at the nursing home or hospital. Still others may find it impossible to be there as often as they would like to be because of distance and other responsibilities. But regardless of how often we are able to be with our parent during this season of his or her life, God will enable us to:

Watch—Of course, we need to keep a watchful eye over the care our parent is receiving even from long distance, but we cannot allow our anxiety to consume us. God has His people stationed everywhere. One or more of those "strangers" may be God's provision for ministering to your parent in a way you cannot. We also need to watch and be open to the ways God may be providing a stranger to minister to our own needs. I still remember my dismay over having to choose a doctor from a list of names the nursing home provided. I didn't know any of them. But God did! He led me to a doctor who was incredibly supportive and compassionate.

Wait—on the Lord to renew your strength (see Isa. 40:31). Trust in His promise to give "power to the tired and worn out" (Isa. 40:29 TLB). Even when you cannot feel His presence, He will be with you and your loved one.

Pray—when you can, if you can. Sometimes we don't know how to pray. Other times the pain may be beyond words we can form into prayers. But God knows our hearts and our frame. Give Him those burdens that have become too heavy. He will carry them—and you.

NURSING CAN

BE HEALING

I can do all things through Christ who strengthens me.
Nevertheless you have done well
that you shared in my distress.
—Philippians 4:13–14 NKJV

My greeting of new patients was usually a heartfelt smile and a warm handclasp followed by, "We're happy to have you with us." The dreary figure with downcast eyes, tears coursing down both cheeks, suggested a different approach.

"I can see that this is a very difficult experience for you, and I do want to help. Here, let me take your coat, and we can sit over on the sofa and talk about what makes you sad."

Slowly her sad eyes looked into mine. "They didn't want me anymore. I made too much trouble for them. They sold all my things, except this." Nervously she twisted her wedding band. "They don't care what happens to me."

A director of nursing service dare not be judgmental. I didn't know the particular circumstances that led her to our door. Her medical records would follow. But the Lord knew and a quiet prayer filled my heart.

Show me, Lord, how to help Mary feel Your presence. Make us all patient with her and loving so she will feel You are with her.

—Margaret I. Miller

When I Grow Old

When I grow old—
too old to know my name,
and where my head must rest,
or how I came
to rest it where it lies . . .
when I have come
to that mute crossroad
where the soul has spun
too many webs
to spin again—
please . . . smile,
and touch me with
your voice a little while.
Oh, never wonder
if I hear or see,
for all the sounds of God
will speak to me.

—Judith Deem Dupree

WHERE ARE YOU,

GOD?

"'When did we see you sick or in prison
and go to visit you?'
The King will reply, 'I tell you the truth,
whatever you did for one of the least
of these brothers of mine,
you did for me.'"
—Matthew 25:39–40 NIV

O h, God," I cried, "where are You?"

I had just returned from my harrowing weekly visit to the nursing home where Mother had been living, or rather, dying, for the last several years. Putting Mother in there had been devastating to the whole family. Intellectually, I knew it was the right decision, but my heart was overwhelmed by guilt, anger, doubt, and grief.

How I hated these visits! Not only was it painful to see Mother's gradual decline into total senility, but she was surrounded by other pathetic elderly people who lined the corridors calling out plaintively. Each week it was a struggle to make that visit. Sometimes I simply couldn't face it, which only added to my guilt.

People to whom I turned for comfort failed to understand. Oh, they sympathized, but their pity was not what I needed. I needed God, but He seemed nowhere to be found.

Then one day I happened to mention to a friend that I was searching for God in that nursing home. "If I could only find Him," I said, "I might be at peace."

"The Lord is in those beds and wheelchairs," he said quietly. "When you visit your mother, you are visiting Him."

My question was answered.

Lord, help us always to see You in the sick and aged that we might minister to them as unto You.

—Nancy Templeman

WISDOM

FOR DAD

*If any of you lacks wisdom, he should ask God,
who gives generously to all without finding fault,
and it will be given to him.*
—James 1:5 NIV

I poked my head into my father's room in the nursing home where he had been for the past four months. Dad sat in his Gerry chair reaching for things visible only to him.

Usually Dad welcomed me with a hug and brief whimper as if to say, "I'm so glad to see you!" Today he stirred when I reached down to hug him, but he sat stiffly, head down, eyes closed. I recognized his behavior as his signal to me that something was wrong.

Taking a closer look, I was alarmed as I noticed that my dad's feet were bare and very swollen. Two quarter-sized, infected sores covered his arch bones.

"We need to pray great prayers," he whispered.

Not gangrene setting in, I worried.

The nurses couldn't tell me the cause of the sores, only what kind of treatment they would give.

Why are so many things going wrong? my mind questioned. Silently I prayed, *Lord, show me what to do. I feel so helpless.*

Dad began to ramble with interesting words but couldn't complete a thought. A dementia-like illness had slowly fogged his mind and drained his energy. In his better days, when Dad would tell a story, he held his listeners' peak interest — especially mine. Now I tried to fill in the blanks and dig for answers. He tried so hard too. We were both frustrated, but the effort drew us closer.

I waited for some heavenly wisdom; mine was not enough. I thought about checking Dad's shoes in the closet. I found both tongues folded under in deep creases. These had irritated his tender skin.

With the help of some extra roomy, soft slippers and prescribed medicine, the sores gradually healed. I rejoiced at God's faithfulness.

God had answered Dad's cry for help through His wisdom. He fulfilled His promise in James 1:5. I knew that I could count on God's wisdom for future problems Dad and I would face.

Father, we give You thanks for the gift of Your wisdom in our lack. Teach us to remember to ask.

—LaVel Reichle

READ ME

ANOTHER STORY

*"Give, and it will be given to you. A good measure,
pressed down, shaken together and running over,
will be poured into your lap.
For with the measure you use,
it will be measured to you."*
—Luke 6:38 NIV

I know this is my idea. Reading is supposed to help pass the time. This book is about something we both enjoy. But while my mouth forms the words on the page, my thoughts run over the list of things I need to get done.

Dad's health has been steadily declining. I still can't get used to seeing him stuck in bed, gasping for breath. It hurts to watch him suffer. There isn't anything I can do to heal his body. I want back the vigorous, active man who is my dad. My voice drones on. *Why did I decide to do this?*

Dad starts to laugh. The character in the story is caught in a humorous situation. My laughter joins his. Together we remember similar circumstances. Somehow the laughter helps us both.

When I continue with the story, Dad starts to doze. My

mind wanders back in time. I remember the afternoons he turned into celebrations just by coming home in his gray pickup truck. He'd climb down from the cab and swing me up over his head. Of course, it wasn't all so idyllic.

I smile as I remember the times our strong personalities clashed. Dad had always been a strong support for me even when I didn't recognize or want it. His being there, no matter what, was enough. What will I do without him?

An awareness steals over me as if the Lord has opened a curtain. The joy of being able to give back to someone who has given to me enlivens my soul. It feels good to be sitting here reading. I ask myself if the undone errands were really important.

The answer is no. I am pleased to be spending the morning giving Dad a break from the physical and emotional pain of his chronic illness.

I pause. This time together is also a break for me from the physical and emotional stress of a far-too-hectic schedule. As I am giving to my earthly father, my heavenly Father is encouraging me by caring for my needs as well.

Thank You, Lord, for reminding me that when I give I also receive.

—Sandra Allen Lovelace

LITTLE PAYMENTS

ON A BIG DEBT

*"But when you do a kindness to someone,
do it secretly."*
—Matthew 6:3 TLB

I was thirty-six years old with children of my own before I really knew how much my mother loved me! The discovery came one day when my parents were visiting from Massachusetts. Dad and Mumzie (we'd called her that ever since my first son was born) always did things around the house to make life a little easier for us. Today Dad was tinkering in the garage while Mumzie ironed clothes in the basement.

"It's almost as hot today as it was the year I went to summer school in Florida," I said.

"It was hot working at the hospital that summer too," Mumzie said. Then she caught her breath and a sheepish grin spread across her face.

I looked at her quizzically. As school nurse in the little town where I grew up, she should have had the entire summer free from work.

An explanation seemed in order, so Mumzie continued.

231

"When you were in college that summer, I worked at the hospital—but I never wanted you to know it." Then she laughed. "You can't imagine how hard it was to never mention anything about the hospital in my letters."

Mumzie had forfeited her vacation to work at the hospital to earn money for my college expenses. "I had no idea you were doing that," I stammered. "Why didn't you tell me?"

"If I told you, I knew you wouldn't go to summer school," she said.

Many years later, after my children had graduated from college, it became my turn to show her a special brand of love. In her late seventies, Alzheimer's eroded her mental faculties till she no longer recognized either me or my dad. Finally her illness necessitated full-time care in a nursing home. But still I could show her my love in the little tasks I could do for her. I was grateful when I could trim her nails or help her eat. They were little payments on a big debt that could never be repaid.

Thank You, Jesus, for giving us the opportunity to show love to those who have loved us. Thank You for Your sustaining grace.

—Faye Landrum

A WHITE

PORCELAIN CUP

Blessed be the God and Father of our Lord Jesus
Christ, . . . who comforts us in all our tribulation, that
we may be able to comfort those who are in any trouble,
with the comfort with which we ourselves are comforted.
—2 Corinthians 1:3–4 NKJV

Can you think of any food your mother might enjoy?"

The doctor's question was simple enough, but his eyes betrayed his concern. Two weeks earlier, he had operated on Mother. Despite his initial assurance that he thought he had "got it all," we soon realized something was wrong. Mother was not healing properly. She could not face any of the nourishment we tentatively offered to supplement her intravenous diet.

Now, rummaging in the cupboards at my parents' home, I find canned soups. Cream of tomato! Suddenly I remember how Mother used to bring me that when I was sick as a child. Its bland warmth was so comforting, along with the cool cloths she spread across my forehead and words of reassurance she murmured over me.

How simple the world, and our relationship, had

seemed then! The memories contrast sharply with some of our more recent times together before Mother got sick—times strained by my struggle to establish a separate life as an independent adult. Necessary struggles, yes, and surely common to many mothers and daughters but oh, so painful to recall!

My reflections are interrupted as my eye falls on a small porcelain cup—white, with gold trim. Why, Mother gave me soup out of that very cup when she brought it so many years ago! I take it off the shelf, marveling at its delicate grace. Then I open a can of tomato soup, heat it up, pour it into a thermos, and bring it, together with the little cup, out to the car.

Back at the hospital, I approach the bed. "Look, Mother, tomato soup. And see, our special cup." She looks at it, recognition lighting her eyes. "Try some," I urge. "Just a little."

She reaches out, her frail arm dragging the tubes, to take it. She sips. "Oh, that's good," she sighs.

The doctor is watching by the bedside. He smiles approval. My father, sitting in the corner chair where he has been keeping his long vigil these last two weeks, allows a tentative look of hope to cross his eyes.

Mother has finished. "Would you like some more?" I ask. Miraculously, she nods.

As I pour the second cup, something remarkable occurs. From somewhere deep inside, I sense a strong, quiet love rising up within me to dissolve—forever, it feels—the painful memories of Mother's and my struggles over the years. Is this my love for her? Hers for me? God's love for us all? Can such distinctions even be made?

As she takes the cup from my hand this second time, she smiles weakly. I smile back. In my heart, a prayer of joy bursts into being. *Thank You, Lord. Thank You for the gift of Your amazing love.*

Father, we thank You for nurturing us over the years and for enabling us, when our loved ones suffer, to give back to them the comfort that they, and You, first gave us.
—**Elise Chase**

JESUS

LOVES ME!

*He gives strength to the weary
and increases the power of the weak.*
—Isaiah 40:29 NIV

Alyce has become quite an evangelist," Mother told a visitor one day. She was *not* complimenting me. Although she'd been active in her church for years, she was puzzled when I tried to share my faith with her.

An only child, I had failed to convince my octogenarian parents to move near me in New Jersey or to enter a retirement home. Strong and independent since her mother died when she was yet a child, Mother had insisted on remaining in Illinois and caring for Dad, whose Parkinson's disease led to frequent falls.

One day Dad fell backwards down the stairs, knocking Mother down. She broke her hip. He died within twelve days. Deeply depressed, she never recovered from the fall.

With full-time care, Mother remained in her home where, in small town fashion, friends and neighbors flocked to visit. And I, a fearful flier, commuted frequently one thousand miles.

How I dreaded each trip! I could hardly bear to see Mother incapacitated. For years we'd been best friends. Exuberant over life, she had initiated jaunts to museums, zoos, and shopping centers. We'd put together puzzles and played games. "We never run out of things to do," she'd always said. But now she was a weak, dependent invalid who'd beg, "Don't leave me." Her tears broke my heart. Once again she was a child without a mother. And I, accustomed to clinging to her for emotional strength, had lost my mother too.

Miraculously, God carried me through those difficult months. The prayers of my friends undergirded me. And each morning my devotionals and praise tapes helped me feel God's Spirit. But how could I help Mother?

"My life is ruined," she bemoaned one day.

"God has plans for you," I replied.

"Do you think so?" she asked, her brown eyes filled with doubt and fear.

One morning I felt a strong urge to play a tape for her. But it made no sense. She did not know the praise songs. And, quite deaf, she would not understand the words. Nevertheless, I held the tape player by her ear and sang along. She did not protest, but somehow I had hoped for more.

And then, suddenly, Mother's voice joined with mine. "Jesus loves me! This I know, for the Bible tells me so. Little ones to Him belong; they are weak, but He is strong."*

I'd forgotten that song was on the tape. Mother had

taught it to me years before. Through those familiar words, we connected. Like motherless "little ones," we were weak. But His strength was sufficient.

Mother died in her sleep soon after that visit. I still miss her terribly. But I cherish the memory of our singing together like little children those words of assurance that God loved us both.

Dear Lord, help us to feel Your strength and show us how to share it with those whom we love most.

—Alyce Mitchem Jenkins

*"Jesus Loves Me," William B. Bradbury.

ALL I
CAN DO

My little children, let us not love in word
or in tongue, but in deed and in truth.
—1 John 3:18 NKJV

You beg me to take you home. You warn me over and over that if I don't, you will die.

I think of the times I thought I would die if I didn't have that new something—the latest fad. I didn't know it hurt you to say no. I didn't understand the lack of money or the other reasons why it wouldn't have been good for me. Now you don't understand when I must tell you no. You don't realize how many hands you need to care for you. At home there are only my two, and not enough money to hire all the others it would take.

You don't remember how heartbreaking it is to say no when all your being cries out to say yes. So I must harden my heart to your pleas. I cannot take you home. All I can do for you is love you.

You shout for me to get you up. You shake the side rails and call my name again and again. You are so tired you can barely stand up, but you are determined to go, go, go—anywhere but here.

You claim they have beaten you, but there are no bruises. You say they have left you alone for hours in the dark, but as I arrived, I saw a nurse leave your bright sunny room. So I just say, "Go to sleep," the way you did when I was an overtired child seeing unnamed monsters in the darkness of my room. I cannot ease your fears or stop your hurt. All I can do for you is love you.

I don't like to see you uncomfortable and confused. I don't want to remember you as you are now. I want my memory to hold only the gardener in the sunshine, the hunter climbing the hill. But I will get into my car and come to sit with you for there may be that one little thing I might do to ease your discomfort—that one time my presence may make a difference—although I know all I really can do for you is love you.

Dear heavenly Father, when words cease to carry any meaning, please give me the strength and courage to go on loving in deed.

—**Helen Kammerdiener**

240

WHEN LIFE IS
FULL OF STRESS

In my distress I cried to the LORD,
And He heard me.
—Psalm 120:1 NKJV

This isn't the robe I wanted! Why can't you do anything right? My sons will bring what I need when they come," Mom shouted, tossing the robe aside.

"I'm sorry! Why am I expected to do everything?" Confused and ashamed of my reply, I turned toward the window to hide my tears. I need not have bothered. Mom was fussing at the nurse.

My husband had heart bypass surgery two days after Mom's stroke. He was home, and I'd had to put Mom back in the hospital. My once thoughtful mother was now demanding and bossy. Since she was unpleasant to be around, my brothers didn't visit. They all wanted to re-member her the way she was before her stroke.

There are few situations that resurface sibling conflicts more than caring for an aged and ill parent. *Lord*, I prayed silently, *I should be home taking care of my husband. Help me deal with the rage I feel toward my brothers.*

Caretakers often hear how they should do this or that from those doing nothing. Now I was doing it to myself.

I felt someone tug at my arm. Mom stood looking up at me, her eyes clear. "I thought you knew," she said. "I thought you knew."

"Knew what, Mom?"

"Why I always ask you to do things for me. It's because I know I can count on you." She hugged me.

For a few minutes, the Lord lifted the curtain of fog confusing her mind. It was long enough to ease the distress filling my soul. The curtain suddenly dropped; her mood changed back to shouting at the nurse.

But the resentment was gone toward my brothers. God allowed me a brief glimpse of how Mom trusted me. I knew He would be with me and give me strength to care for my loved ones.

Thank You, dear Lord, for hearing our cries of distress and for Your ever-present Spirit in the midst of family conflicts and illness.

—**Marie Butler**

CLOSER TO
THE TRUTH

From the fullness of his grace we have all received
one blessing after another.
—John 1:16 NIV

My mother and I were never bosom buddies. Growing up as an only adopted child, I never felt estranged, but neither did I feel close. We were opposites in our likes and dislikes. I was considered a bookworm, more ready to write than sew or housekeep. I'm not sure what my mother's hidden dream was for me, but mine was to have her love me as I really was.

In her older years as a widow, we helped her move to a senior retirement apartment in North Carolina. I envisioned her busy with friends and activities in her golden age. It never happened. First, there was a sudden onset of dementia. Then, as I looked for living arrangements close to me in Colorado, she had a paralyzing stroke.

Now I take along photos when I visit so she can remember her grandchildren and their spouses. I push her chair down the nursing center corridors. I point out flowers like ones she has grown and children who are visiting who look like her grandchildren. I pat her hand when she seems tired or out of sorts.

This isn't what I had planned for her later years, but out of this pain has come a reminder for me that our blessings may not be what we have sought. I care for my mother very much, and I have realized how much she's cared for me. In different ways, we have been dependent upon each other as I am sure God intended.

My mother, I've discovered, had a difficult childhood and youth, often without love and support. God has given me insights I might never have had about her in other circumstances. Knowing her life, I understand my own much better.

The Lord has shown me how to provide for her. Her face wreaths in smiles when I come, and I do not feel alone.

Dearest Father, thank You for not abandoning us but through Your grace constantly reminding us of Your love and caring. Help us to see others with Your eyes of love.

—Vickie Ferguson

HIS

PRESENCE

But thou art holy,
O thou that inhabitest the praises of Israel.
—Psalm 22:3 KJV

As I stepped off the elevator at the nursing home, I could hear her. "Help! Help! Help!" Her strong voice projected well despite her ninety years. The constant, repetitive call, "Help! Help! Help!" carried down the corridor piercing my body and cutting through my soul.

"Hello, Mother," I greeted her as I entered the room "How are you today?" The gleam in her eyes, a short smile, and a nod of her head was her response as she lay in her bed, her frail frame making an outline through the covers.

Taking her hand gently, I said, "The eighty-mile drive from home went well, despite the rain. It's a light, gentle rain, a welcome rain. The boys are fine, busy with their work . . ."

Mother was quiet as she absorbed who I was. But then her tired body began its familiar cry, "Help! Help! Help!" It was a quieter call, but just as persistent, punctuating my family news.

Taking her well-worn Bible from the bedside stand, I read from Psalm 71, "O God, from my youth thou hast taught me, and I still proclaim thy wondrous deeds. So even to old age . . ." (v. 17 RSV). Her cries for help lessened, then stopped for awhile. But I read too much and the "Helps" interrupted again.

In the bottom dresser drawer were copies of the old green hymnal. I took the one in which my sister had marked Mother's favorite hymns. I began to find the tune of the first one listed. "That's not right," corrected Mother. She then softly sang the melody correctly.

"Okay, I'll try again." And with the right melody I sang through the old Swedish hymn she loved. No cries for help came while I sang through hymn after hymn. Mother closed her eyes to listen. The peaceful presence of the Lord filled our time of praise in song. After awhile Mother slept, having been comforted by our loving heavenly Father as we praised Him in song.

Thank You, Lord, for Your presence with us. Help us keep a song of praise always on our lips.

—**Karen Gronvall Larson**

ARMS

AND HANDS

She sets about her work vigorously;
her arms are strong for her tasks.
—Proverbs 31:17 NIV

This precious little lady I call Mama sits in her wheelchair day after day and works vigorously with her arms and hands. She uses them to push her wheelchair around, but mostly she uses them to smooth her hair in a constant combing motion as her hair gets thinner and thinner. Mama also uses those hands to quilt on the Afghan that keeps her warm. Her hands shake steadily from Parkinson's disease when they're not combing or quilting.

I think about those sweet little arms and hands, and I realize that they've never been idle. They've always worked vigorously and lovingly.

Those are the strong arms that held me and loved me and took care of me when I was a baby and then a little girl. Those are the hands that patted me lovingly and wiped my tears away.

Those dear hands made pretty dresses for me and embroidered bunnies and flowers on them. They carefully scalloped the hem of my first long dress for a piano recital and placed a fresh sweetheart rose at each point. How lovingly those hands worked!

Those hands very carefully kept the books for my daddy's store. And those arms and hands cooked countless tasty meals for our family and kept an immaculate house for us.

My mother used those arms and hands to draw my babies to her breast and to cuddle and love them as she had me many years before. They were older and wiser arms and hands, but still strong, vigorous, and loving.

Now those arms and hands are old and frail. They shake and show their years. But the love that nurtured those strong, vigorous hands remains in my mama's heart.

Thank You, Lord, for the love and strength You taught me through Mama. May my arms and hands be strong, vigorous, and loving like hers.

—Mary Lynn Davis

JUST

YOU WAIT

For thou art my hope, O Lord GOD:
thou art my trust from my youth.
—Psalm 71:5 KJV

Just you wait until I become your mother—then I'll be your boss!" The childhood scene played out mentally as I looked at Mother in her wheelchair. With tousled hair and sparks flying from her eyes she was "laying down the law" about conditions in the nursing home. Now it was she throwing the temper tantrum, and we were both finding out who was the real boss.

"They restrain you in your wheelchair because you fell on the rocks when you broke their rules and wandered outside," I tried to explain to her.

I thought back to the fiercely independent woman she had always been. At the depth of the early 1930s Great Depression (when she was in her early thirties), she was forced to make the transition from Protected to Protector. Her husband and her father died just months apart, leaving her no insurance, no training to earn a living, and the responsibility of caring for herself, her mother, and her two children. She lost most of her material possessions, but she never lost her faith in God's protection and provision. When I worried about money, she always said, "God will take care of us." And He did.

The awful day came when hardening of the arteries to her brain began taking its toll in ways that required nursing home care. Picking at the sleeve of her sweater, she would look into her own private space—a space which I could not fathom—and murmur, "I wonder what is to become of me? I don't have enough money to pay my bills."

Then it was my turn to comfort her. I would remind her, "God took care of you in times worse than this. He will not leave you nor forsake you now." And, once again, He was faithful.

The ten years of her declining health (including two and a half years in a nursing home) were dark, dismal days. A piercing shaft of light through that darkness was the blessing of renewed faith.

Dear Lord, thank You for watching over us so lovingly. May I never forget Your loving presence, protection, and provision.

—Gwen Northcutt

A BETTER
PERSPECTIVE

Finally, brothers, whatever is true, whatever is noble,
whatever is right, whatever is pure, whatever is lovely,
whatever is admirable — if anything is excellent or
praiseworthy — think about such things.
—Philippians 4:8 NIV

Mother made me angry many times. When I was growing up, I'd cook supper after school. I'd do my best. Sometimes I'd have the table set and the meat, potatoes, and vegetables all ready to serve when Mother came home from her job at a downtown department store. She'd come in, hang up her coat and hat, take one look in the kitchen and say, "Where's the salad?" My glow of pride in having everything ready would be crushed. Once again I'd failed to please my mother.

These memories and others bothered me when I visited Mother in the nursing home. In her declining alertness she'd call me by my sister's name. She rarely called me Karen. It hurt.

Finally, after tears, time, and sharing with my sister and

friends, I was able to forgive her. I asked God's forgiveness too.

Mother still didn't call me by name, but I could love her and remember the good times—how she taught me the things she loved:

> To sing from the heart in praise to God.
> To bake rye bread—
> > rich and chewy,
> > cardamon rolls—
> > > fragrant and light,
> > > melt-in-the-mouth pie crust—
> > > > delicate and flaky.
> To garden, inside and out,
> > digging in dirt and flowerpot
> > > watching God grow luxuriant green
> > topped with lovely blossoms.
> To watch and listen for beautiful birds
> > bursting with joyful song
> > > to our heavenly Father.
> She passed these on
> > without a structured program.
> She loved these, lived these,
> > taught these—without trying.

Thank You, Lord, for loving us, forgiving us, and helping us forgive those who have hurt us.

—Karen Gronvall Larson

A BALLOON

FOR MOTHER

"Man looks at the outward appearance,
but the LORD looks at the heart."
—1 Samuel 16:7 NIV

Nurses loved coming to my mother's hospital room filled with flowers from friends and family. "You're such a joy to be with," one said. "I wish my mother would talk to me the way you do."

The day came, however, when Mother lay staring—ignoring her beloved flowers—her eyes dark and round, her fingers clawing at the food tray.

The specialist transferred her to another floor. New nurses, already overburdened, did not give her the help she could no longer ask for. She looked as desperate as I felt.

"Lord," I prayed, "Mother devoted her life to helping others. Now she's the one who needs help. I can't be here all the time. How can I get her the attention she needs?"

His answer came in a strange way. I found myself easing snapshots from Mother's photo album: the cute little five-year-old sitting on the steps with her sisters, the spritely eighth-grader beaming in her white dimity dress, the working girl clowning with her friends, the bride and groom jumping waves at the seashore, the mother, the businesswoman, the grandmother, the hostess, the knitter.

With the library's photocopier, I made a collage that I taped on Mother's door, next to her chart. I tied balloons to the head of her bed. I left a basket of peaches on her nightstand with a note: "Help yourself."

They did. They also combed her hair, fluffed her pillows, and—I could tell by the chart on the door—checked on her more frequently. Through photos from the past and balloons from the present, God had given my mother a way to "speak" again.

Heavenly Father, help us to find ways of honoring our loved ones—Your children—as they make their way from the prisons of their aged bodies to the joys of Your eternal kingdom.

—Ruth Harrison

&

ANOTHER
HUG

*Husbands, love your wives, just as Christ loved the
church and gave himself up for her.*
—Ephesians 5:25 NIV

I heard soft steps outside of my home office door. I turned
to see my wife, hesitantly coming into the room. She was
trying not to cry as she blurted out, "Mom—Mom called
and . . ." Then the tears came.

I turned off my typewriter, stood up, and gave her
another hug. Carol held on and sobbed as she told me of
another stinging telephone call from her aging mother.

My wife and I are middle-aged newlyweds. Her mother
is elderly and recently fell. The fall could have been worse,
but it was bad enough for someone her age. After a short
stay in a hospital, her mother was transferred to a nursing
home.

Carol's work schedule is demanding, long, and stress-
ful. Ten- and sometimes twelve-hour days are not unusual
as she deals with the law, the land, and people who want
to transfer ownership of the land. Added to her hectic
professional work calendar is the burden of assisting her

mother and the aunt with whom she lived. Visits to the nursing home and telephone calls to doctors, social workers, and insurance people consume a lot of her time.

But what can I do? We are still in the process of getting to know each other as newlyweds. That has its own set of problems and challenges. I turn to the Scriptures for help and find, as I often do, that the Holy Spirit leads me back to Jesus. He gave Himself for the church, and that is what He wants me to do for my wife.

But what does that mean? Since I work at home and she works out of the house, I do more of the dusting, vacuuming, dinner preparations, and dishes. Carol would like to spend large amounts of time puttering in the yard; but since she can't, I do more of that now. I make myself available to go with her when she travels on business. Whenever possible, I try to put her needs first.

Jesus wants me to have more compassion and patience for her. She needs more hugs. She does not want my advice as much as a listening ear. That is really hard, especially when I'm used to giving advice, but with His help I'm learning.

Jesus, You died for Your church. If necessary, help me to die for my wife, giving myself up for her.

—**John B. Calsin, Jr.**

A SPOONFUL

OF PUMPKIN PIE

I will . . . make the rough places smooth.
—Isaiah 42:16 NIV

How's my mother today?" I asked the nurse at the desk.

"About the same. Still won't talk or respond. Perhaps you could coax her to eat her dinner?"

"Sure," I replied halfheartedly. "I'll try."

Mama didn't hear me as I entered her room. She stared out the window, motionless except for the hand that endlessly plucked the bedsheet.

"Hi, Mama!" I bustled to her bedside in a cloud of animation. "Happy Thanksgiving! It's really cold out today. You're lucky to be in a nice warm room." I rambled on in my best "let's-cheer-up-Mama" voice. I couldn't blame her for not responding.

A nurse shuffled in bearing the dinner tray. We exchanged the usual trite commentary on how Mama was going to enjoy her dinner.

I removed the gray metal cover from the plate, revealing Mama's Thanksgiving dinner. One section held two thin slivers of turkey dryly nestled against a scoop of tweed that vaguely resembled stuffing. Another section had a tiny mound of white that looked more like spackling compound than mashed potatoes. Half a slice of bread was hermetically sealed in plastic, while the final section of the plate contained a square of tan congealment charaded as pumpkin pie.

I suddenly envisioned Mama, young and pretty, wearing her "company" apron, proudly carrying a platter of turkey to the dining room table. Next she served the stuffing that she prepared before sunrise, every ingredient lovingly chopped and sliced by hand. Then came the mashed potatoes, the sweet potatoes, the salad, the rolls.

I tried to brush the vision aside as I raised a spoon of mushy potatoes to her lips. Obediently, she opened her mouth. Spoon after spoon, she quietly received her Thanksgiving dinner.

Would this be our last Thanksgiving together? I wondered. In a way, Mama was already gone. Her body pitifully held on for life, but the essence of her was gone. She no longer even knew me.

"Look, Mama, pumpkin pie!" My cheeriness caught in my throat as I spooned up a fragment of the sickly concoction. My hand trembled as I raised the spoon, but Mama's lips were locked tight. Surprised, I glanced up. There, looking out at me from the depths of her sea-blue eyes, was Mama—not the mere shell of my mother, but her real self, alert and full of recognition. A tiny tear tipped over the edge of her eye. I dropped the spoon of uneaten pie and gently put my arms around Mama's fragile shoulders. She breathed a tiny sigh and relaxed in my arms. And for one sweet moment, her hand stopped plucking the bedsheet.

Father, thank You for one last Thanksgiving with Mama and for smooth moments through life's rough places.

—**Eileen Anderson**

IS SHE
STILL LIVING?

"In My Father's house are many mansions. . . .
I go to prepare a place for you, . . .
that where I am, there you may be also."
—John 14:2–3 NKJV

Rarely, these days, does anyone ask about my mother. Occasionally someone may ask, "Is your mother still living?"

I step back and ask myself, "Is Mom still living?" It's a strange question to ask because she never died. Yet, in my mind's eye, my true mother is gone. She died eight years ago when we moved her into a rest home. Since then, gradually, she has declined from an active, strong woman to a wisp of a stiff body. Her mind is gone, and there is no response to her environment.

But I keep visiting her. The nurses assure me that the last sense to leave the body is hearing, so I tell her about springtime and how the flowers are bursting into bloom. I place the freshly picked bouquet before her eyes, but she doesn't even blink. I tell her of the wedding which is foremost in our thinking. "Mom, your granddaughter is getting married. She chose her dress and looks so pretty." Then I choke up and can't continue.

I play her favorite songs on the tape recorder and reach out to touch her. There is no response. I feel like screaming. "This isn't my mother! Where is the caring, reaching-out-to-meet-you mother I once knew? Where is the fun-loving mother with a gleam in the eye, the smiling mother?"

Then a thought occurs to me. It's not strange no one asks about her. She's ninety-one. Most of her friends are gone. Many are in the same position as she. If not that, they don't get around much.

As I place pictures on her wall, I think of the myriad flowers she cultivated and shared with others. She entertained guests with merry laughter and she was just the age I am now. My mind jolts me to reality. "What memories am I creating in my children? My grandchildren?"

I saw it happen. I saw my mother's world getting smaller and smaller until she withdrew into herself. Now she is placed in a wheelchair, but she seems to prefer lying in a fetal position in bed. Soon her body will be free to soar to her Creator.

I repeat a Bible verse to her that she taught me as a child. It was the message given by Jesus to His followers: "In My Father's house are many mansions . . ."

Yes, dear Mother, you have given me the single most important thing in life any mother can give her child—a faith in a living God. I want to live by that faith, and someday I will be reunited with the true mother I once knew.

Dear Father, instill in me the appreciation of who my mother is, was, and shall be. May I never lose sight of the faith she instilled in me so that I may share heaven with her eternally.

—Celia Lehman

S e a s o n s

Like a November leaf,
colorless, brittle, curled,
she waits
in the nursing home
for December's wind
to blow.
Her hope:
heaven's springtime—
to bloom again,
like a verdant, ever-new
green leaf.

—Betty Kossick

THROUGH
HIS EYES

[Growing in grace] they shall still bring forth fruit in old age; they shall be full of sap [of spiritual vitality].
—Psalm 92:14 AMP

I watch their faces come and go. Some smiling, some grim, some resigned to facts they'd rather not know. It is not easy leaving their loved ones here—entrusting their care to a stranger like me.

I see anger, guilt, fear, rippling through their eyes like waves of the sea. Do I dare to go? they seem to say. Do they really know the right way to fix Mom's hair or tie Dad's tie? Will they be gentle when confusion comes and the questions fly? Will they laugh when my parents cry at being here all alone? Or will they understand it's hard not to be on your own? Will they take the time to listen when she tells that story for the hundredth time of where she used to live? Will they be impatient when he soils his clothes or drops his food, or will they forgive?

No, it is not easy leaving their loved ones here with me. What an awesome responsibility! I'm not sure I'm equal to the task—that I can be and do all that they ask. Yet, Lord, I know these older ones more than friends or family can.

Lord, please take my hand. Let me see them through Your eyes. Let me not despise the work You've given me.

Help me to look beyond the shaking hands, the dimming eyes, to the ageless spirit that lives inside. Help me to bless and touch and love as if You were here . . . as I whisper in their ears, "Jesus is here; don't be afraid. We'll take good care of you."

—Cheryl L. Zimmerman

Possessions

Her life, in boxes
in my spare room.
She asks for something every visit,
something in a bottom box
in a far corner.
I find the time,
feeling no resentment,
so grateful she still remembers the boxes
and me.

—Marsha Owens Hood

LEARNING
TO LEAN

The eternal God is your refuge,
and underneath are the
everlasting arms.
—Deuteronomy 33:27 NIV

This was a special day. I got up early for the 400-mile drive to visit my mother. The route was one I had taken many times.

Throughout the day memories of other visits drifted across my mind. Some were happy, like the Mother's Day Tea. Mom's memory was suddenly activated to remember happy tea parties with grandchildren years earlier. How we all enjoyed the light that came into her eyes!

Other memories were colored gray and still brought pain. These were times when her confusion, anger, and agitation had obscured the pleasure of reunion. No wonder I found myself repeating a simple prayer, "Dear Lord, please make this visit a blessing."

Arriving in town, I quickly phoned a brother. He advised me not to expect too much. Earlier in the day, Mom had been unable to recall having an older daughter. With that in mind I hurried to the nursing center that is now her home.

As I walked in, a look of guarded remembrance crossed her face. Quickly using my name, I announced my arrival. Stepping into her well-honed hostess role, she began introductions. She was glad to see me even if she wasn't sure of our connection.

I led her to a secluded area. Holding her hand, I listened as she happily talked on blending past generations and events in a montage of confusion. Pausing briefly she began, "My Mommy knows where I am. She thinks this is a good place for me to be. But I'm glad you could come and see where I am."

Then, leaning against me she added, "Now I can take new courage."

The silence of a hallowed moment followed. Tears fell as I sat in recognition of a loving Father's sweet presence and the answer to my prayer.

Thank You, Father, that Your arms are strong enough to enfold both Mother and I.

—Rosemary Browne

SONG IN
THE NIGHT

"But no one says, 'Where is God my Maker,
who gives songs in the night?'"
—Job 35:10 NIV

My father's bypass operation had not gone well. During surgery, his blood pressure dropped to zero, and for several minutes, he was dead. The surgical team revived him, but the shutdown of his whole system had induced a massive stroke which left him in a coma.

Family hurried to Dad's bedside. A pastor offered his sympathy. Nurses avoided questions. One doctor apologized for the hospital's role in prolonging my father's life.

"What's the matter with everyone?" I asked my husband in the middle of an especially critical night.

He shrugged but said, "If you want, we'll get in the car and go see him right now."

"But it's 2 A.M. The nurses won't let us in."

"Yes, they will," my husband answered.

Since the drive took an hour one way, I wanted to be sure. I put on my most conspicuous cross, then told the ICU staff, "We've come to pray." No one objected!

Apparently, that's what we really were there to do. My husband and I prayed over my father, his room, the hospital, and staff. I don't know exactly what we prayed, except that it was whatever the Lord Himself brought to our minds.

We left ICU that night with a sense of peace. We felt certain Dad would be okay and he was. Not only did he eventually awaken from the coma and regain the 98% vocabulary he lost, but a few months later, he went home—without a walker. That's been over five years ago!

I suppose our prayers helped my dad, but I know for sure they helped me! As my husband and I sought God our Maker, He gave us peace. He gave us prayers to pray. He gave us songs in the night.

Dear God, thank You for sustaining those who watch and those who pray for parents. No matter what lyrics come with our situation, we know that You alone are our song and strength.

—**Mary Harwell Sayler**

&

IN HIS
NAME

And whatever you do, whether in word or deed,
do it all in the name of the Lord Jesus,
giving thanks to God the Father through him.
—Colossians 3:17 NIV

Both of our mothers were wasting away in nursing homes. It seemed overwhelming. At least my mother resided close enough that I could continue to do for her, but my mother-in-law lived hundreds of miles away.

My husband dreaded the visits. Each encounter exhausted him as he searched for a spark of recognition in his mother's eyes. This woman who for sixty doting years proudly said, "This is my Johnny," saw only a foreigner now. Nor did she remember his brothers. Surely she'd remember the name of her husband? No. She didn't even respond to Johnny's prayers. The once familiar voice no longer comforted her. Only strangers took up residence in her memory.

The "angel" aides and nurses assured us that no response was Mama's usual reaction except for continual hollering of incomprehensible sounds. And she stared!

The ominous scenario frustrated us, haunting us long after each departure. Yet I felt sure there must be some way to break through the dark tunnel of non-memory.

Then I heard music playing. "Mama," I asked, "do you remember when you used to sing in the church choir?" Her eyes blinked. The stare eased.

Her lips quivered as I began to sing "Jesus Loves Me." Johnny brightened, "I think she's trying to sing!" he exclaimed.

And she did! She sang out all the words, not mumbling, but clear and distinct. The simple words of a pristine praise to Jesus pushed aside the spiderwebs of confusion, allowing remembrance to penetrate through lost thoughts like sunshine through a fog. For awhile Mama was again a member of the choir, probably looking down from the loft to see if her three boys were behaving.

Father, though there are more exquisite hymns of praise to glorify Your name, it was a simple child's song expressing the name of Jesus which opened a lost mind to praise You again. May the name of Jesus always keep my mind open to You, I pray.

—**Betty Kossick**

THE GIFT

OF GLADNESS

"But he never left himself without a witness;
there were always his reminders—
the kind things he did such as sending you rain
and good crops and giving you food and gladness."
—Acts 14:17 TLB

There is a 1922 high school annual with a breathtaking picture of my mother among the faculty. It shows a dark-haired beauty. Her hair is piled high on her head in front and bound with a large bow at the nape of the neck. Her features are regular with large, limpid, brown eyes. Her expression is one of entrancing innocence!

I love that picture! I want to wave it in front of friends who knew her only after age had taken its toll. I want to insist, "This is my *real* mother!"

No matter what the ravages of time did to my mother, the person I saw was beautiful. Her hair turned white and lost its sheen. Her big brown eyes got cataracts and became dim. Her body stooped, shook, and needed an arm to lean on. Other people saw the elderly lady. I saw her courageous acceptance, her struggle to "not be a burden."

Perhaps my gift to her was to see the real person—the beautiful person. The giving of gifts was not one-sided. I remember the night she gave me my gift! I treasure it!

She was in the hospital. I entered her room and stood beside her barricaded bed. Her limp body was just an inert lump under the sheet. Usually her eyes would be closed; her hair fanned out on the pillow. I would talk to her a little while to bring her around. This time I said softly, "Hello! I love you! You're my mommy!"

Her eyes slowly opened. They focused on me. Her mind replayed what I had just said. Then she gave me the quietest, deepest gift she could give. She said, "I love you. I would love you even if you were not my daughter!"

Her gift of love touched my heart with gladness. I was loved as only a mother can love a daughter. More than that, I was loved as a person!

Father God, with all my heart I thank You for the gifts You give us. The gift of provision. The gift of gladness. How very kind You were to create us, Your children, with the power to love. May we share with others the love You give to us.

—Anne Clack

THE BREAD
OF LOVE

Listen, my son, to your father's instruction
and do not forsake your mother's teaching.
They will be a garland to grace your head.
—Proverbs 1:8–9 NIV

When I was a kid, Friday was always special. It was the day Mom baked fresh bread for the family. I'd run home from school and hang around her kitchen just to smell the sweet dough as it turned into golden loaves of bread.

One Friday I pointed to her old-fashioned gas oven with its vault-like, porcelainized-steel door and said to her, "I know I can smell it, but how do I know there's really bread in there?"

Mom looked a bit surprised. "If you can ask a philosophical question like that, you must be growing up," she said with a twinkle in her eye. "But, I'll tell you," she continued, "it's a matter of faith. Like believing in God. You can't see Him, but you know He's there. Always loving you. Always watching over you."

Then came the Friday I really learned about God's love. It was hard times for Dad, and a serviceman from the gas

273

company came to shut off our gas because the bill wasn't paid. I knew it was humiliating for Mom to open the oven door and show the serviceman the still uncooked dough lying in the two glistening bread pans.

"Would you please wait a little while before turning off the gas, so my family can have bread tonight?" she implored.

The serviceman dropped his head and mumbled, "Sure, lady." Red-faced, he walked from Mom's little kitchen, climbed into his truck, and waited.

An hour later, the serviceman came back and walked down to the cellar. Mom and I heard the cold clank as he attached his wrench to the gas valve and turned it off. When he came upstairs, he grimly approached Mom. "I have something for you," he said, and then handed her a bill. "When it's paid, I'll come back and turn on your gas."

Mom smiled and folded the bill carefully. She put it in the pocket of her apron and said, "I have something for you too."

She picked up a carefully wrapped package and handed it to the serviceman. It was a warm loaf of fresh baked bread. The serviceman's face lit up. "Thank you," he said, "and God bless you!"

That was years ago. And now, when I look down at Mom lying in her hospital bed, I long to talk to her, but she can't speak. I want to tell her how much I love her, but she can't hear. Only her hands let me know she still thinks of me. They constantly move, kneading the dough and shaping the loaves.

Thank You, Father God, for giving me a mother who opened my eyes to Your great love and compassion.

—Bert Clompus

GOING

HOME

Weeping may endure for a night,
But joy comes in the morning.

Psalm 30:5 NKJV

I've never been able to understand why so many women get motivated to houseclean in the spring. To me, warm breezes and the melting of winter's snow and ice signal that it's time to get back outdoors, not to stay inside and do spring-cleaning. Actually, to be honest, housecleaning is never high on my priority list, but this past Christmas I did put forth a good effort before my daughter came home from college. It's amazing how her earlier criticism about our "messy" house motivated me.

As our parents prepare to move to a new house, as Candy Abbott's mother put it (see p. 281), some even more important housecleaning needs to be done by them and by us.

Of course, our primary concern is what their future address will be. Do they know Jesus as their Lord and Savior? I'm so grateful I had the privilege of leading my mother to the Lord ten years ago. Knowing she would spend eternity with Him made it so much easier to face her homegoing.

But what if your parent is not a Christian? What if, even worse, they've repeatedly rebuffed your attempts to share the Gospel?

I don't have any easy answers, but I do know that the Lord longs for your loved one to come to Him even more than you do. Keep praying, keep believing. God still works miracles!

Whether or not your parent knows the Lord, there is some housecleaning you need to encourage them to do. If they haven't already done so, they need to get their financial and legal affairs in order and write a will. But even more important, is the need to clean up relationships that may have gotten out of order. If there are relationships in your family that are estranged, do what you can, prayerfully and sensitively, to bring reconciliation before it's too late. Peace cannot be made with a corpse, nor will your parent know the comfort of the restored relationship after he is gone.

Think through your own relationship with your parent. Ask forgiveness for ways you may have hurt him. Choose to extend forgiveness to him for ways he may not even know that he has hurt you. If your parent is too confused to understand the words you need to say, say them anyway. And even if he is in a coma, remember that hearing is the last sense to go.

Finally, if your family is not a family whose vocabulary includes those three special words, "I love you," now is the time to say them. Don't waste any more time. And each time as you say the words, release your parent into the hands of the Lord and know that joy will come in the morning for you and for him.

LIKE MOVING
TO A NEW HOUSE

*Though outwardly we are wasting away, yet inwardly
we are being renewed day by day. So we fix our eyes
not on what is seen, but on what is unseen. For what is
seen is temporary, but what is unseen is eternal.*
—2 Corinthians 4:16, 18 NIV

Your dad called," my husband said as I breezed through the door after a hectic day at work.

"Mom's test results?" I asked, my eyes searching his face for some hint of encouragement.

Drew was not smiling. "It's not good. Your dad thinks it would be best to tell you in person."

The unknown hung ominously in the air as we drove the forty-five-minute distance, mostly in private thought. My fingers picked at my cuticles. *Don't fidget,* I told myself. Through misty eyes, I stared at the bare bones of February trees as they sped by. *They look dead, but they're not*, I reminded myself.

Weak knees carried me to the front door, up the stairs, and into the dining room where Mom and Dad were waiting. The news was worse than "not good." It was terrible. Hospice would be called immediately.

My brothers and I tried courageously to digest the magnitude of Mom's condition. She looked so frail, so exhausted, as she asked us to help her lie on the couch. "I'll just listen for awhile," she sighed and closed her eyes. Mine began to water and suddenly I couldn't talk. My brothers' questions tumbled out. As our constricted vocal cords sought to come to grips with this, our conversation was interrupted by soothing words from the couch.

"You know," said Mom, "I think this is harder on you than it is on me. It's kind of like moving to a new house. The person who's moving away has a lot to look forward to—new surroundings, new friends, new possibilities; it's an adventure. But it's hard for the people left behind in the old neighborhood. All they have is an empty house and some memories. They're lonely, and for them it's sad. Don't feel sorry for me."

In the weeks to come, as her health declined, Mom got ready for her "journey." She discarded some excess baggage—like regrets from second grade. She packed up some unresolved issues in her mind—things that were too deep for us to understand. During long, sleepless nights, the voice of Tennessee Ernie Ford serenaded her with songs like, "Lord, I'm Coming Home." Often, during the days just prior to her death she would remind us, "Better get ready, we're moving."

Lord Jesus, thank You for the hope that we can move in with You when our earthly bodies wear out. When visible

282

and temporary things loom over us, remind us to look
beyond the tangible to the unseen things that are everlast-
ing.

—Candy Abbott

Re-Creation

And God will say,
"Let there be light.
Let the darkness of evil no longer reign.
Let there no longer be thorns and thistles,
    sin, death, and decay.
Let there be a new heaven and earth.
Let the home of God be among His people.
Let all tears be wiped away.
Let the thirsty drink from the spring
    of the Water of Life.
Let all creation rejoice
    in the salvation of the Lord."

—Marlene Bagnull

THE CLANGING
CYMBAL

*But he said to me, "My grace is sufficient for you, for
my power is made perfect in weakness."*
—2 Corinthians 12:9 NIV

I hung up the phone and began to tremble. My body had
absorbed the doctor's words. My mind had yet to take them
in. "Your mother has inoperable cancer."

I had to go to her. But what could I say that would be
of any comfort? Ah! I'd share my news with her.

"Guess what, Mom," I began.

My mother's eyes flashed icy sparks. "Don't tell me
you're pregnant again." She gave a snort of disgust. "Just
when I need you too. After all my sacrifices . . ."

I realized it was pain and fear that were lashing out at
me, but that didn't make the sting any less.

All my efforts to help my mother were met with storms
of abuse. I returned her harsh words with gentle answers.
Still my favorite Bible passage became a clanging cymbal
in my ears. "If I speak in the tongues of men and of angels,
but have not love . . ." (1 Cor. 13:1 NIV).

Hard as I tried to feel loving, my affection for my mother shriveled like bacon in an overheated pan.

I shopped for her. I cleaned. I hired baby-sitters so I could spend hours with her in doctors' waiting rooms.

Fatigue burned in me like a fever. My first-grader's school papers got no more than a glance. I tumbled my toddler into bed without his bath. The clanging grew louder. *I'm failing in everything.*

When I took Mom into the hospital, neither of us would admit the end was near. Concerned about her salvation, I seasoned small talk with evangelism.

"What do you mean, *saved*?" Mom snapped at me. "I was never lost."

I winced, and her eyes pleaded with me to understand.

I kept quiet after that. I sensed that Mom's suffering would eventually break down the prickly barriers that separated her from the Lord.

As I suffered with her, the Lord began to get through to me. *Entering into someone else's pain, this is love.* It was a different kind, not warm, cuddly affection.

This new kind of love required spiritual muscles I had not yet developed. My weakness drew me toward the Lord's strength.

Sitting in that small island of silence amid the hum and clatter of the hospital, I began to understand. The love the Lord demands of us is the love He longs to pour into us.

Father God, help us to remember to call upon Your grace so that our strength and patience will not fail when others need us.

—Beverly Eliason

R e p a y m e n t

She changed my diapers,
I change hers.
She fed me,
I feed her.
She helped me walk,
I do the same for her.
She shielded me from the world,
as I do her.
I tried her patience,
as she does mine.
An opportunity
to say thank you.

—Marsha Owens Hood

WHO WILL FIX
THE BROKEN THINGS?

The Lord is close to those whose hearts are breaking.
—Psalm 34:18 TLB

I bring Mama home from the hospital to a half-lighted house. Immediately, I call my two little girls to me and we sit on the love seat in front of the fireplace. I tell them the truth—that Grandpa's house-body is all worn out; that Grandpa will soon leave his house-body and go to live with Jesus.

We talk about how Grandpa asked Jesus to be his Lord and Savior those many years ago and how glad he will be to see his mother and baby brother in heaven. Ellen bows her head and lets her hair fall forward over her face. But Jenny sits straight and tall while her eyes become great, deep wells of tears.

Mama comes into the room and goes to Jenny. "It's all right to cry, Jenny," she says softly.

The child throws herself against her grandmother and sobs out, "I don't want Grandpa to die."

"But we don't want to keep Grandpa here and make him hurt, do we, Jenny?" Mama asks.

"No," Jenny sobs, "but who will fix all our broken things?"

Indeed. Who will now be the mender of broken toys and kitchen gadgets, of fractured chair legs and go-cart wheels? And who will fix our broken hearts? Oh, God! Are You aware of our grief?

The warmth of the fire spreads throughout the log house—a house unusually silent for one sheltering three adults and five children. And then I am aware of the warmth of His love; the love of One who bore our griefs and carried our sorrow. It permeates the air. It is He who will fix the broken things.

Thank You, dear Lord, for Your constant nearness when we traverse the valleys of grief.

—**Coleen Frye Barber**

MOTHER'S
CHRISTMAS GIFT

*And God has reserved for his children the priceless gift
of eternal life; it is kept in heaven for you, pure and
undefiled, beyond the reach of change and decay.*
—1 Peter 1:4 TLB

Mother has only a few weeks to live," I sorrowfully told
my husband, Dewey. "Her doctor told me she may not even
make it through Christmas."

My heart was breaking. Mother had always, even during the Great Depression, tried to make Christmas special.
Even when we were desperately poor, she managed to
provide small gifts—a pretty embroidered handkerchief, a
box of dominoes, a tiny toy truck, or stocking caps she had
crocheted with yarn unraveled from worn-out sweaters.

Now Mother lay critically ill in the hospital. I couldn't
bear to think of her spending her last Christmas on earth
in a lonely hospital room. The only solution was to bring
her to our home.

Mother's first Sunday with us was wonderful. Our
children clustered around her. My sister's family came to
visit, bearing gifts for all. We sang carols and everyone

enjoyed a delicious dinner. With light snow sifting down all day, it truly was like Christmas. By evening we all were exhausted, but what a glorious time we had.

Yet my plan to have Mother home for Christmas was futile. The following week fluid started building up in her lungs and she began to fail. We had no choice but to return her to the hospital. Two weeks later she went home to glory.

"Why, Lord?" I cried. "Couldn't we have kept her only a little longer? She enjoyed that last Sunday with us so much. Would such a short time have made that much difference to You?"

Gently God helped me to see my selfishness. Mother was suffering far more than I realized. How could I have wanted to keep her chained to a bed of misery? No, God knew what was best.

Christmas morning I said to Dewey, "Can't you picture her now? She's received her best Christmas gift ever. God gave her a brand new body that will last for all eternity. And she'll never suffer again."

Give us peace, dear Father, when You call our loved ones home to You. Freed from all pain and sorrow, we know they will be waiting for us to join them some day in a joyful eternal reunion.

—**Georgia E. Burkett**

I'VE NEVER
DONE THIS BEFORE!

I will bring the blind by a way that they knew not; I will
lead them in paths that they have not known. . . . These
things will I do unto them, and not forsake them.
—Isaiah 42:16 KJV

I left home when I was fifteen and hitchhiked 1,000 miles
to San Antonio. In looking for a job, I kept seeing the
phrase, "Experience Required." How I hated those two
words. After all, what kind of job experience could a
fifteen-year-old produce?

Three years later I stood and watched while my wife
had a baby at home. We both had to go into this new arena
of life without prior experience.

We had three kids in a row. No one had even advised
us how to raise children; we experimented with what we
had. And then, when they were all teenagers, we took in
two other teenagers. I'll never forget the trauma I felt as I
cried out to God, "I've never raised teenagers before! I
need help!"

And so it went through life. I kept entering new fields
of battle and challenge—never having covered that turf

291

before. Then along came "old age." Not for me, mind you, but for my parents. It was little things first. And then greater burdens, challenges, responsibilities, and yes, even greater blessings.

My dear old dad has been in school for eighty-nine years. He's never had to die before, but he's in the hospital on the threshold of trying his last new experience on earth.

I've never had to care for the elderly before. It's not easy to learn as you go. It's not always fun to get on-the-job experience. But there's one consolation. My mother and mother-in-law are both eighty-three. My father-in-law is ninety. They are all in good health now, so I still have time to perfect what I've been learning.

After I've gotten these three "graduated" to heavenly experiences, I can proudly display a certificate of accomplishment on my office wall. It will read: "Experienced parent of four parents."

Dear Lord, I've never walked this way before. The path is crooked and sometimes steep. Darkness shrouds my way. Please take my hand and guide me over uncertain ground. Shine the light of instruction before me. And when You cannot give me understanding, help me to trust—to simply trust and obey!

—**David Dodge**

A SHARED

CUP OF COFFEE

Length of days is in her [Wisdom's] right hand.
—Proverbs 3:16 NKJV

Is there enough coffee for you to have a cup too?" asked
Mother. There was, and I sat on the sofa near her recliner.
Together we watched an inane cooking program on TV
and sipped coffee.

The day before we thought we were losing her. Several
other times in the past year she seemed to be slipping away
from us. Each time I'd pray that the Lord would take her
home if she couldn't return to health. A full span of
eighty-seven years, a beloved husband already in heaven,
and now a total dependency on her family made heaven
seem a very attractive alternative. Yet now she was enjoying this simple activity, and it was less than twenty-four
hours after the last crisis.

I thought of the controversy surrounding doctor-as-
sisted euthanasia. No wonder it sounds like an act of
compassion to terminate a life which seems to be useless.
Mother is in no pain, but many are trapped in pain and a

terminal condition. How can we resist the thinking that we know when life should end?

I changed my prayer after thinking these thoughts. One of the greatest dangers in all areas of life is to think we can play God. How do I know what God is doing in Mother's inner being through these situations? How do I know what He is doing in the lives of each of her loved ones? How did I know she would recover and enjoy a cup of coffee with her daughter?

I do know one thing. Grandchildren have shared phone conversations because of Grandma. Strained relationships have been forgotten in their common concern. How can I know what other positive results are being accomplished through Mother's life—fragile though it is?

Whether the life of the unborn, or the life of the aged is at stake, I am not God. I cannot say when the miracle of birth or the passage from this life into eternity should occur.

Lord, Mother is in Your loving hands. Help me to accept whatever You allow to happen and accept it with total peace—the peace You give.

—Joan Corrie

HER
HANDS

*For this reason I also suffer these things; nevertheless I
am not ashamed, for I know whom I have believed and
am persuaded that He is able to keep what I have
committed to Him until that Day.*
—2 Timothy 1:12 NKJV

As I sit by Momma's bed in the early hours of morning,
her frail hand grips mine and she softly asks, "Is it time for
my shot?"

"It'll be a while, Momma," I answer.

I study her tired face. She struggles to hide the pain for
the medicine no longer works. I know her three-year battle
with cancer will end soon.

My first memories in life are of Momma. She was there
to pick me up when I fell. She brushed away the tears and
soothed the hurt. Daily she guided my two sisters and me
through the maze of growing up. In our eyes, Momma
could solve any problem.

Each night her hands folded in prayer as she placed us
in Jesus' care. At the break of each new day she renewed
her faith in Him.

Restless, Momma stirs in her bed.

"Would you like me to rub your back and arms with lotion?" I ask. She nods without opening her eyes.

I pour the warm liquid on and gently massage. She sighs, smiles, then folds her thin hands on her chest and begins to pray.

Her time draws closer—hours, perhaps a day, but her belief in Jesus Christ gives her comfort. Momma knows whose kingdom she's in.

I blink back tears and join her, "For thine is the kingdom, the power, and the glory forever. Amen."

Thank You, Lord God, for giving us Jesus Christ. Because of our belief in Him, Momma and I will reunite in heaven. We'll join hands and never be parted again.

—Helen Luecke

HEAVEN
BOUND

*The Lord is . . . not willing that any should perish
but that all should come to repentance.*
—2 Peter 3:9 NKJV

My dad had gone to church as far back as I could remember, but he did it with the same enthusiasm as brushing his teeth. After I found Christ as my Savior, I realized his churchgoing was perfunctory; he had no personal relationship with Jesus. My husband and I frequently made this a matter of prayer and looked for every opportunity to tell him about the plan of salvation. But Dad always sloughed off our attempts. Not a denial, just an indifference.

When Dad was seventy-five, doctors discovered one of the arteries in his neck was almost obstructed. They advised immediate surgery. Afterward Mother called to say everything had gone well. The next afternoon, however, she called again. "Your father has had a small stroke," she said, her voice quivering. "He's paralyzed on one side. He keeps asking for you."

My knees felt like day-old Jell-O as I told her I'd take

the next available plane to Florida. I threw a few clothes in a suitcase and was ready to leave for the airport the minute my husband got home. Friends of my parents met my plane and brought me to the hospital. Dad had been transferred out of intensive care and was in his own room. He was awake and seemed so relieved to see me.

The next morning as I was helping him bathe, I said, "Dad, what you need is the Lord."

For the first time in his life, my father was powerless to execute control. His left side was limp. He couldn't even turn over by himself. "I guess I need something," he muttered.

I had his full attention as I explained to him that we are all born as sinners and need to turn to Jesus for forgiveness. He held my hand and prayed with me to ask Jesus to come into his life.

That day in the hospital meant so much to me, but it wasn't until eight years later that I experienced the full impact of it. That was when the supervisor at a nursing home called to tell me my father had died during the night. My first thought was, *He is with Jesus now.* What a wonderful assurance to know someone you love is in heaven!

God, in His great mercy, wants all of us to be in heaven with Him—but only He knows for sure who will be there. We may find many surprises when we get there. Our loved ones may have made a decision about Jesus when they were very young, or a doctor or nurse may have helped them find the Lord during the very last minutes of their life. God loves us with a love greater than we can comprehend. He will provide an avenue to His home.

Father, thank You for giving us Your Son who died that we might live forever.

—**Faye Landrum**

P r a y e r f u l l y

Mother's back may be bent
in weakness, yet her face
turns upward with certain hope.
In her halting journey,
her spirit stirs steadfast in faith.
When I see her veer toward the
final valley, I bring close my lamp,
a lantern fueled with aching love,
lit by Christ, the light of the world;
the One who tenderly sees us home.

—**Charlotte Adelsperger**

A TIME
TO HEAL

There is a time for everything, . . .
a time to be born and a time to die, . . .
a time to kill and a time to heal.
—Ecclesiastes 3:1–3 NIV

For many in the high school class of 1970, the final bell of the school day signaled the end to classroom drudgery and the beginning of play. But for me, school and the responsibilities surrounding my mother's illness left little time for play. Being shy, I didn't miss the frivolities that absorbed my peers, but I did long for the rapport some seemed to share with their mothers.

Mommy's illness intensified our already distant and strained relationship. Although I conscientiously shared household chores and custodial responsibilities, my actions were based more in duty than love. In the latter stages of her illness, Mommy required a colostomy and ileostomy, and during what was her final home visit, I found myself alone with her.

Hearing noises from her sickroom and feeling alarmed by what might be a medical emergency, I rushed in. I was

300

surprised to find her struggling to get out of bed. "Mommy, what are you doing?" I asked. "The doctors said you have to stay in bed."

Exhausted, she rested a full minute before she could respond. When she spoke, her voice was at once quiet and commanding. "I need to go to the bathroom, child. I'm trying to change these bags, and that's not the kind of thing I want to bother anybody with."

I was stunned. Her words and waif-like appearance awakened my discernment, demanding I recognize her person, and her illness. She was my mommy. She was hurting, and I could help her. I *wanted* to help her. I quickly made the changes to the bags. When I returned, she was crying softly in her pillow. I sat on her bed and stroked her hand, understanding instinctively that she felt diminished by her helplessness. For the only time I can remember, my mother and I talked.

I can recall few of the particulars of that twenty-five-year-old conversation. But somehow, without actually saying the words, Mommy imparted her sorrow and anger at facing death so early. She communicated her faith in God, her love for me, and her need to be released from her battle for life. I gave her permission to weep over her losses and let her know I'd be alright after her death. In me, she found a loved one who was willing to release her.

She died within weeks of that conversation. Years afterward my heart ached over our relationship. But Jesus' love has helped me discard useless regrets. I know that both Mother and I did our best under difficult circumstances. I loved my mother. That simple knowledge has been a key to freedom and healing in my life.

Thank You, Father, for Your healing touch of love. You are now and always will be Jehovah Rapha, the God who heals us.

—**Marilyn P. Turner**

RESTING ON
THE PROMISES

"My grace is sufficient for you, for My strength is made perfect in weakness."
—2 Corinthians 12:9 NKJV

Why doesn't the Lord take me home?" Dad said mournfully.

I had heard this many times over the past few months. Dad could no longer be involved in the pastoral ministry he loved. He was lonely without Mother, who had gone on to heaven. His frail body was in pain and depression clouded his mind.

But my father had always been the tease, the one to see the amusing side of everything. I missed his sense of humor and wished I could make him smile again. So this time I tried the light touch. "Dad, you wouldn't want to get to heaven before God gets the roof on your mansion, would you?"

He stared at me as though I were a creature from outer space speaking an unknown language. I bit my lip. I had said the wrong thing—again. Remorseful, I laid my hand on his. "I know you are anxious to be with the Lord," I assured him, "and one of these days He will gather you up in His arms and you will suddenly find yourself in His presence."

His eyes brightened and he relaxed. Soon he slept.

I breathed a prayer of thanks, knowing that he and I could both rest on the promises of God.

In our weakness, God promised that we can depend on His strength. He has promised that His grace is more than enough for our need. Not only is this a promise, He is stating a fact.

And He promised that He will never leave us nor forsake us.

What more could I ask? His strength, His grace, and His presence are all-sufficient.

Dear Father, thank You that we can depend on Your loving faithfulness.

—Florence E. Parkes

THE

GIFT

Blessed is the man who perseveres under trial, because when he has stood the test, he will receive the crown of life that God has promised to those who love him.
—James 1:12 NIV

Dad lay desperately ill in a hospital bed; I so wanted to give him a gift. But what he needed most couldn't be found on any shelf of any store.

Or could it? I anxiously scanned a store display. A small, but thick photo album caught my eye. It was covered with the warm colors of harvest fruits and flowers. I flipped open the cover and discovered each four-by-six-inch page was a clear plastic pocket. "Perfect," I thought aloud.

As I purchased the album, I could tell it would be just the size for him to hold. He tired so easily. Though Dad would not discuss his prognosis, he hinted concern by setting goals. First Tom's birthday, then Thanksgiving, then Mom's birthday . . .

When I got home, I found a pad of paper with a border of roses and forget-me-nots. I cut a piece in half and found it fit perfectly in the pocket. On the top of one sheet, I wrote the date and began a letter to my dad. "I want to celebrate each day with you by giving you a gift, the gift of words to build you up! We're starting today!"

The book grew faster than expected. I included the date, an encouraging Scripture, and a short note in my daily entry. Throughout each day my mother, siblings, relatives, and friends also added to the pages. Some wrote about Dad's faith and example, some about special memories, some about everyday events. Others wrote words of thanks and encouragement. His grandchildren drew pictures. What was held back by mouths, splashed out from hearts onto the pages.

Dad's book had sixty-eight entries. He reached one goal, Tom's birthday. He received one medal, the Paul Harris Fellowship Award. But more than these, I feel in my heart he reached the ultimate goal—heaven. He received the highest honor, the crown of life.

We will always treasure this book, my dad's legacy. I hope when the book of my life lays open, it will show whatever I faced, I pressed toward the mark. I reached the goal, heaven.

Father God, please give us strength to endure our trials and press on toward the mark.

—Elaine M. Englert

LEANING

ON A CORNSTALK

"Look! You are trusting in the staff of this broken reed, Egypt, on which if a man leans, it will go into his hand and pierce it."
—Isaiah 36:6 NKJV

The cornfield lay under a heavy frost. Like a shimmering sea of steel, sunlight bounced off it in brief blinding flashes. I eased Daddy into his chair by the window.

"This house is too hot," I muttered as I backed through the laundry room door, careful not to spill the sloshing basin. Getting to therapy had become a real hassle. I drooped over the agitating washing machine. *I can manage,* I said, encouraging myself.

Later that morning, I explained to the therapist: "I'm an only child and live in Oklahoma. My dad is alone. When can I take him home with me?"

"Your father is dying," he told me.

Yes, I thought, *but I'm strong. I can manage.*

With an unsteady hand, Daddy reached up to me. His eyes searched my face for reassurance.

I pulled him close. "You can lean on me, Daddy."

My husband called that evening. I listened to my ten-year-old. Her voice was fragile and whining. "When are you coming home, Mom? I need you."

What could I say?

I turned the egg and buttered the toast just the way Daddy liked it. But Daddy couldn't eat. "This is garbage!" he accused.

My stomach turned over. I knew he was scared. I was scared too. Yet, as I scraped food into the disposal, I told myself once again, *I can manage.*

I fell into bed exhausted. Sounds of labored breathing echoed off the walls. I pulled back the warm covers and tiptoed into Daddy's room. The air was stale and heavy.

"Will you help me roll over, honey?" he asked.

One lonely tear dropped off the end of my nose. No one noticed.

I bumped through the darkness toward the family room. Whack! Daddy's walking stick fell at my feet. I caressed its smooth handle as I stared absently across the wind-tossed cornfield.

"He leans on me now," I spoke into the silence. "But God, I'm not a walking stick. I can't even support myself. I feel more like a cornstalk, cracked and jagged under the weight of a winter ice storm." Sinking into a nearby chair, I knew I couldn't manage any longer!

The wind blew. The clouds shifted. Moonlight washed across the wall where a familiar picture hung—"The Out-stretched Arms of Jesus." As I stood to examine it closer, my shadow fell across His hands.

"Won't you let Me hold you?" He seemed to say.

"Yes," I answered.

Love wrapped itself around me with new tenderness, inviting me to rest a while. I did.

Self-reliance can keep you going for a time. Jesus will sustain you forever.

Thank You, God. You don't leave us leaning on a cornstalk. We are safe in Your hands, the hands that were pierced for us.

—Shirley Folwarski

FIVE

SPECIAL MONTHS

They shall obtain joy and gladness,
And sorrow and sighing shall flee away.
—Isaiah 35:10 NKJV

In August 1991 my mother's chemotherapy quit working and we knew we were looking at the beginning of the end of her life on earth. Off and on she had stayed with us during the past year, but now she would be in our care continually.

When we left the doctor's office that day, she asked in a straightforward manner, "What did the doctor say? Don't keep back anything from me."

I didn't know how to break the news gently, so I simply said, "You only have weeks to live."

I needn't have worried. Mother was ready for the news. She began to rejoice. "Oh, I'll soon get to see Jesus! I'll get to see my other loved ones."

If anyone in your family has received a huge promotion, then maybe you can understand the jubilant feeling we had anticipating her soon arrival in heaven. The sense of celebrating a promotion was unmistakable. We rode down

Rainbow Boulevard (the actual name of the street) crying for joy.

I'm glad we didn't know then that she would suffer nearly five more months and that her already weakened body would continue to waste away to a mere seventy-five pounds.

God knew I needed an unmistakable sign of His all-sufficient grace. One night, at the beginning of those five months, I awakened and went downstairs to pray. Too worried to pray, I thought, *What if the doctor is wrong and she has several more months to live?* I didn't know if I could handle a long illness. Mingled with the pain of watching my mother suffer and the pain of losing someone I loved dearly, was the frightening thought of having to acquire nursing skills. Even combing someone else's hair was "not my specialty," as my mother put it.

Suddenly God spoke to me a line from an old song, "I will fear not the future and dread not the foe."* My fears vanished. If her illness lasted five or six months it didn't matter. God would provide.

And provide He did. It was as though God Himself orchestrated her care. It seemed so natural to learn how to turn her in bed and to acquire other basic nursing skills I thought I could never master.

One day I was overwhelmed by the thought, *I'm taking care of one God will embrace to Himself and care for affectionately all eternity!* I recognized it as a high honor. "It's a privilege to take care of you," I began to tell her.

God took her to Himself on January 5, 1992. Now she's

being cared for by Him. I'm thankful I had the privilege for five months.

Thank You, Father, for being our refuge, and that underneath were Your everlasting arms.

—Aletha Hinthorn

Present Tense, Future Perfect

He doesn't know me,
the long-ago little girl who remembers
my father, sent to quiet me,
standing at the foot of my double bed,
rhythmically lifting the mattress
to watch me bounce with giggles of delight.
Now I stand at the foot of his bed.
Shrunken in fetal position,
turning in on himself,
the chrysalid monarch waits to fly free,
and with God's promise,
I wait with him.

—Marsha Owens Hood

LEARNING
TO RECEIVE

"For everyone who asks receives and the one who seeks will find and to the one knocking, it will be opened."
—Luke 11:10 (author's translation)

The tricky thing about caregiving is the blindness that can become its occupational hazard. When we give, we can forget to receive. When I was busy caring for my father who was suffering from a terminal illness, I found it difficult to receive.

One night the phone rang its deafening message. My husband answered. I could make out only a vague idea of the message. "My father's dead?" I said, hoping that in saying the words, it would somehow brace me for the news.

"No, it's *my* dad!" he said. "He's just been rushed to the hospital." We couldn't both go with no one to watch our babies so I said good-bye, promising to pray. He promised to call as soon as he got to the hospital. No more than ten minutes later the phone rang. I answered, expecting to hear my husband's voice. Instead, my older sister told me, "Karen, Dad's dying."

A friend of the family was sent to watch my children. Meanwhile, the phone rang again. My husband told me his father had passed away. I told him about my dad. We were numb. Our fathers died twenty minutes apart!

All during my dad's illness I had counted on my husband being there. Now he was with his family; I with mine. I'll never forget that week of viewings and funerals. I felt like a wet washcloth.

The people from our church were tremendous. Many came to both viewings and several came to both funerals. They sent cards, flowers, fruit baskets. Some watched our children. Others brought food. This flood of love came pouring into my life. All reserves gone, I had to let it in.

"It is more blessed to give than to receive." But for me, an over-functioning adult, God had to teach me that it is more blessed to receive.

Gracious God, help me to receive graciously the love others have for me. You have sent them to show You care. Help me not to be so busy that I forget my own basic needs that You have placed within me as a person whom You have created in Your image. Keep me tender by accepting the love and kindness of others.

—Karen L. Onesti

DO WHAT
YOU CAN

*"She did what she could. She poured perfume on my
body beforehand to prepare for my burial. I tell you the
truth, wherever the gospel is preached throughout the
world, what she has done will also be told, in memory
of her."*
—Mark 14:8–9 NIV

Don't ever do that to me again," Mother said as I
removed her coat and placed her in her favorite chair. I had
just brought her home from the hospital.

"Whatever did I do to upset you so?" I asked, pretending
total innocence. I was quite fearful that she meant exactly
what I thought she meant.

Mother lived with me as cancer of the stomach
destroyed her body. Three days prior to this an ambulance had taken her to the hospital. While there, they
administered blood transfusions and intravenous feed-
ings. The doctors said that they had done their best but
there was nothing more that could be done for her.
They sent her home, but we were all aware of the
situation.

"You know very well what I mean," Mother continued.

"You're only prolonging my misery. The next time, please, just let me go."

I gave her my word but didn't realize the agony of keeping that promise. The emotional turmoil was devastating as I watched her waste away, both of us totally helpless.

When the "next time" arrived, I had to decide what to do. Should I renege on my promise and call the ambulance? As I cared for Mother, she'd look at me and shake her head no.

As I prayed, the Lord gave me the strength to do the best that I could. I simply could not force her to live in pain. Sometimes I'd go for a walk so she would not hear me crying. I loved, cared, and prayed for her. That was all that I could do. The rest was up to the Lord and His timetable.

It's been a few years since Mother died and I am at peace. The blessing of comfort and freedom from regrets is beyond expression. The present may be very difficult, but later on it's always a blessing to look back with confidence, knowing that I did all that I could.

Father, I know that You love the care-giver just as much as You love the cared-for. Help me to do all that I can so that I may hear Your "well done."

—**Grayce L. Weibley**

WISDOM FOR
THE ASKING

If any of you lacks wisdom, he should ask God, who gives generously . . . and it will be given to him.
—James 1:5 NIV

Pol—ly," my father-in-law called as I waved his wife into a van to go to the airport.

I closed the front door and went to his bedside. "Polly's not here. She went to Florida for Jackie's wedding," I said, as I stroked his forehead with a damp washcloth, attempting to cut through his confusion and soothe his thrashing.

His responses varied from "Oh, that's right; now I remember," to irrational tirades in which he shouted and tried to climb out of bed to go find her.

The reality of caring for Dad for a week crashed in upon me. I was two hundred miles from home with a list of telephone numbers as my only link to the outside world. Would I know what he wanted or whom to call if he had problems?

"Lord," I prayed, "the rest of the family has confidence in me because I'm a nurse, but I have lots of questions and fears. Please give me Your wisdom."

As I cared for Dad, I noticed his confusion increased in the first hour or two after taking his pain medication or sleeping pills. He seemed calmer and more alert as they wore off. When he asked for his next dose, I questioned him about his pain.

"I'm not really having much pain," he said.

When I explained that the pills might be causing confusion, he agreed to try Tylenol first and to use the stronger drugs only if needed.

The change was dramatic! His disorientation cleared. We played checkers, talked about life and death, and prayed and sang together. I marveled at his faith in God and his will to live despite a diagnosis of terminal cancer. It became a week when we drew close.

Dad died right after Christmas, but he did so quietly and with dignity having prayed for and talked with everyone in the family including Jackie and his new son-in-law who came for Christmas.

Father, even today I thank You for the gift of those final weeks made possible through the wisdom and strength You gave just because I asked.

—**Patricia Souder**

✄

TEARS THAT TRICKLE,

TEARS THAT GUSH

Jesus wept.
—John 11:35 NKJV

It had been building up in me all week. My eyes would water every now and then, but I would change the subject, say something cute, or act strong. If a loose tear should happen to escape and roll down my cheek, I would remind myself of God's inner strength and regain my composure.

Mom set the tone for us. After meeting with the doctor and receiving her "death sentence" (as Dad calls it), she said, "Well, I guess I won't be renewing my magazine subscriptions." Mom was a lighthearted realist, a quiet woman who didn't want any fuss made over her. She was my role model.

Wednesday night at choir practice the news was only five days old—my mother might have days or weeks to live. I thought I was holding up well. I moved with the others to the choir loft to go over Sunday's anthem. I opened my music. The organ began to play. Halfway through the first line, I became aware of the words we were singing. Comforting words, hopeful words, touching words.

My voice cracked. By the time we got to the part about the "everlasting arms," I couldn't sing at all. I just stood there choking back tears as the music swelled around me. *It'll pass*, I told myself. But by the last verse my tears were flowing freely.

"Are you all right?" Connie said, turning to me as soon as the anthem was over. Suddenly her arms were wrapped around me and I was burying my head into her neck like a little girl, sobbing and weeping for what seemed the longest time. The choir was held speechless by my outburst.

The last thing I wanted was to draw attention to myself. Kelly, coming to my rescue, said, "Come on, honey, let's get out of here." She led me downstairs where I sobbed against her breast.

Soon the choir rejoined us. Jim suggested we pray. As the group formed a caring circle around me and prayed, my grief was tempered with peace. I began to understand that Christian fellowship involves receiving as well as giving.

Thank You, Lord Jesus, for Your example of tears as well as strength. Help us to comprehend the importance of vulnerability and the blessing it is to be on the receiving end of comfort.

—**Candy Abbott**

A "YARN"
ABOUT LOVE

*[Love] bears all things, believes all things, hopes all
things, endures all things.*
—1 Corinthians 13:7 NKJV

Mother was not expected to live much longer. But she
never spoke of death as she kept knitting Christmas presents and making plans to see all her family.

One day I took her to the hospital for treatments, and a
nurse told her about a good place to buy yarn at the woolen
mills nearby. Mother talked me into taking her there.

"Are you sure you feel up to it, Mother?" I knew car
rides were painful for her.

"Yes. Let's go now while we're out and I have the
energy."

So we set off in my old Volvo through crowded and
confusing city streets. At one point we found ourselves
driving in circles. Mother held her sides with laughter. If
it hurt, she didn't let on.

At the factory store, we found wool dyed in every
imaginable hue. Mother exclaimed over the colors and
textures. "I get excited just thinking about new projects,"

she said. "Knitting is fun because each pattern is a new challenge. I'd love to make these sweaters." She thumbed through a pattern book, then replaced it on the rack. "After I finish the Afghan I'm working on now, I'll knit for the grandchildren." Her tone of voice indicated there would be plenty of time.

Inspired by Mother's enthusiasm, I selected a cart full of yarns. Waiting in line to pay for them, I glanced at Mother. She stood looking at woolen fabrics. A cloud seemed to have crossed over her. She was frowning. How tired she looked, how thin, how old.

The joy of my purchase vanished. Leaving the shopping cart, I walked over to her. "Mother, here's a chair. Why don't you sit down?"

"I think I will. I guess I should have taken a pain pill this morning, but I hoped I could get by without it."

Returning to the cashier's line, I thought, *What are we doing here?* Suddenly I resented the whole scene: bustling shoppers, busy clerks, long lines. *What is the purpose of all this?* I thought. I made my purchase and walked Mother to the car, feeling sad with the realization that these times with her would come to an end.

Later I watched Mother as she sat knitting a ski cap for my sister. I knew she often prayed as she knitted. The long blue plastic needles kept crossing and interlocking the loops of green and white yarn. In a similar way her prayers were connecting link upon link of loving requests to the heart of God on behalf of those she loved.

Mother loved life and held to it as long as she could.

But even more she loved God and the people He put in her life. That enabled her to endure, believe, and hope to the end.

Dear Father, thank You for showing me that health and length of days are not as important as living and loving fully in the time You have given.

—**Catherine Lawton**

JUST
LET GO

*The eternal God is thy refuge, and underneath are the
everlasting arms.*
—Deuteronomy 33:27 KJV

One day when I was twelve years old, Daddy needed my help. He wanted someone to drive another tractor to the field because his got stuck in the mud. He planned to connect the Farmall with a chain and pull his out.

I was elated to think he asked his "little girl" to do such an important task. But then, I knew I was chosen because my brother was away at camp. I never had been allowed to drive the tractors because everyone thought I was too short to push in the clutch and shift the gears.

As I drove out of the driveway, I felt like I was ten feet tall. But when I started down the hill, my joy turned to fear. A quick glance at some gauges proved that something was really wrong. The needles swayed back and forth. No matter what I did, the old tractor coughed, sputtered, and jerked. The brakes didn't work, so I went faster and faster down the hill. I couldn't even shift into low gear. The gears were locked. The tractor was out of control.

I looked back at Daddy. He waved his hands and shouted, "Don't be afraid. Just let go. Jump!"

Immediately I jumped, and within seconds his strong arms cradled my trembling body. We watched as the tractor continued down the hill and finally came to a stop by hitting a tree.

Years later I stood beside Daddy's hospital bed and watched needles dance back and forth on monitors. Certain body functions were out of control due to pancreatic cancer. Like the old tractor, he occasionally coughed, sputtered, and jerked trying to be released from all that didn't work anymore.

Seconds turned into minutes, and minutes became hours. As I watched his body continue to go downhill, God brought back the tractor incident in my mind. Sweet words of His promises captivated my thoughts, and I sensed a fresh awareness of His presence. His peace, His strength, and a new assurance caused me to focus on heaven. The Lord was waiting with outstretched arms for the moment Daddy would jump from this life into eternity. And, those same loving arms would steady me as I faced the reality of letting go of his earthly life.

Confidently, I took hold of Daddy's hand and in my heart I waved for him to jump. Then I leaned down near his ear and whispered, "Don't be afraid, Daddy. Just let go."

Father, thank You that Your everlasting arms are strong enough to hold us when we tremble and need to let go.

—**Barbara Hibschman**

Mother's Hands

Like the gnarled roots of an ancient tree
Clinging precariously to a windswept cliff,
Your hands anxiously grasp
the sheet beneath you;
I watch, and suddenly I see
it's life itself
you're clutching frantically.
Don't be afraid—your roots,
unlike the tree's go deep
into the rich soil of Christ.
You can let go, but He will not let go of you.
Mother, your pruning's done.
Go, bloom anew.

—Nancy Templeman

TAKING CARE
OF MAMA

For I can do everything God asks me to with the help of
Christ who gives me the strength and power.
—Philippians 4:13 TLB

Until this week, I have striven against it with a vigor born of frustration. "We will try something new and Daddy will get well. We will find out what is wrong, and the winter will pass and he will grow strong in the mountain springtime. We will respect his wishes and not put him in the hospital."

Now I know with sudden finality that God has set the course in a direction different from my choosing. I have cried myself to sleep against my husband's wide chest because I am watching my daddy die, and I cannot stop it.

We brought him home this morning. The words *cancer* and *terminal* are tempered by those of *fastest growing* and *least painful*. Did he know? Is that why he moved Mama here, so that we could care for her? I quail before the thought. I can't take care of Mama. Surely Daddy must know I could never take his place.

"Come into the office on Monday," the doctor says,

"and my nurse will teach you how to give injections—just in case your father does need relief from pain."

"I can't," I protest.

"Yes, you can," is the firm reply. "You can do whatever you have to because you are his daughter and you love him."

Suddenly I am awash with relief. It is not up to me, after all, to look ahead and determine what I am capable or incapable of doing. I can do anything God asks of me with the strength and power of His Son, Jesus Christ!

Mama is functioning with a grace and clarity of mind that amazes me. I know Daddy, nine years her senior, has long been concerned about going first and leaving her alone. As Daddy's strength ebbs away, she is absorbing it.

Yes, I can give injections. And I can take care of Mama. I can do anything God asks me to do—because of love.

Father God, help me to remember that nothing is going to happen today that You and I can't handle together.

—**Coleen Frye Barber**

THE CLOSING
SEASON

There is a time for everything,
and a season for every activity under heaven:
a time to be born and a time to die.
—Ecclesiastes 3:1–2 NIV

Mother is dying by inches. She's slowly drifting away. She says only a few things. I wheel her through the nursing home halls. She's quiet then.

"Rub my back. Oh, my back, my back."

I rub her back over the spot where she's always said it aches.

"Help. Help me."

Her habitual call is like an automatic reflex. But despite that, I inquire, "How may I help you?"

She comes to a higher level of attention for just a moment and seems surprised that someone has heard her call. Without an answer, she lapses back into her favorite position, head in hand. Her body calling again, "Help. Help me." Her mind is in some faraway place.

"When can I go home?" she wails.

"This is your home now, Mother. Only God knows when you can go home to Him," I reply.

Mother is dying by inches. She no longer wishes to eat. It's very hard to watch. It hurts to see her frailty increase and her frame slowly shrink. Only an occasional smile lights up her bony countenance.

It's a season of life, the closing season, when all that used to matter is gone and only the promise of heaven is a bright gleam ahead.

Thank You, Lord, for all the seasons of life. Help us accept them as they come to those we love.

—Karen Gronvall Larson

The February Trail

I hiked with you once down winter trails
With windswept, skeletal trees,
Where you made me feel the April buds
Asleep in those lifeless limbs.
You bore my weight when the path grew steep
And my feet slid from under me.
Now, take my hand and lean on my strength,
I'll help you along the way,
Down this last February trail
That leads to the Lord's blessed spring.

—Beverly Eliason

A DRESS

FOR MOTHER

*Each man should give what he has decided in his heart
to give, not reluctantly or under compulsion,
for God loves a cheerful giver.*
—2 Corinthians 9:7 NIV

Though Mother had become so unsteady on her feet that she seldom left the nursing home, I wanted to buy her a new dress for Christmas. She had always liked pretty clothes, but whatever I bought also needed to be practical.

I like to shop and often go to two or three malls before I choose. This time was different. I went to only one store, and almost at first glance I knew what I wanted.

It was a soft blue crepe—her favorite color and style—with lots of tiny pleats in the bodice. She no longer had pretty clothes and would enjoy wearing it to our family dinner. She might not remember the occasion the next day, though.

I shuddered at the thought that the dress would not be laundered by hand and might be frayed or stained if I ever saw it again. I bought it anyway and did not try to make sense of my purchase. At her age and in her precarious health, any holiday might be her last. Her present was ready weeks before the trip I planned to take from Kansas City to Nebraska.

When Christmas came, she did not open the box and wear the dress. Just before the holidays she fell, hit the back of her head, and suffered a blood clot. Christmas Day she was in the hospital in a coma. She passed away a few days later without regaining consciousness.

There are no malls in the mid-Nebraska town of two thousand, and the weather was typical of December—snow-packed roads, poor visibility, and a glaze of ice. It might have been difficult to find the right dress for her funeral at a time when I was already emotionally drained I was spared that by one of the most "impractical" gifts I ever bought. How thankful I am that I had followed the leadings of my heart, not my head!

Lord, help us to give because we care about others the way You do, not because it always seems to make the most sense.

—**Margaret Primrose**

TOGETHER
UNAFRAID

*For he hath said, I will never leave thee, nor forsake
thee. So . . . we may boldly say, The Lord
is my helper, and I will not fear.*
—Hebrews 13:5–6 KJV

J ust think," said my friend Doris. "Your mother brought you safely into this world, and now you'll be there to help her cross over into the next."

I hadn't thought of it that way. *Birth and death are private things nobody can do for you,* I considered, *but she doesn't have to be alone or afraid when she dies.* I resolved in my heart, Lord willing, to be by her side just as she had always been by mine.

"I want to be with her when she dies," I announced to Dad.

"That's morbid," he said. "You don't need to be here. I can handle it; I've seen lots of people die."

"This is different, Dad. You've never had a part of yourself die before. Besides, it's not a matter of whether or not you can handle it. It's important to me. I'm her daughter and I want to—I need to—be with her."

"Of course I'll call you," he said tenderly. But he didn't have to, because as signs of the final stages approached, I had moved in with my overnight bag.

I was there when Rev. Riley stopped by for a meaningful conversation. "It's like she wants to die," I told him, "but doesn't know how."

"This might sound strange," he said, "but some people hold on subconsciously for the sake of their loved ones. Sometimes it's a good idea to give them *permission to die.* If you get a chance, you might want to say out loud to her that it's okay."

Around four A.M. two days later, in the agony of what would be Mom's last hours, the Lord reminded me of his words.

"I hurt," Mom said for the first and only time I can ever recall.

"I know," I said, wishing the pain could be mine.

She opened her mouth just wide enough for me to put the liquid morphine on her tongue.

"It's hard, Mom. You've never done this before," I said, trying to think of words she would use to comfort me if our roles were reversed. "You're doing a fine job, Mom. You're doing it just right. You don't need to be afraid, you know." She nodded and relaxed into the pillow.

"It's March 20th," I continued. "I know you said you didn't want to die on Drew's birthday, but I had a chance to talk with him about it. He said he would count it a privilege if you would choose today to die."

A tear escaped her closed eyelids, and she attempted a smile. Together we faced her final moments, unafraid.

Lord Jesus, thank You for never leaving us alone. Even if nobody else can be with us, we don't need to fear because You have promised to be there to help.

—**Candy Abbott**

V i c t o r y

> I see your tears
>   and cry
> I feel your pain
>   and ache
> I know your faith
>   and rejoice
> You have won.

—**Marcia Krugh Leaser**

THY WILL
BE DONE

"This, then, is how you should pray:
'Our Father in heaven . . .'"
—Matthew 6:9 TEV

Every evening my mother would quietly go up to her room, sit in her chair by the window, and pray. As a curious five-year-old, I tiptoed into her room one night and asked, "Mommy, why do you pray?"

My mother smiled at me, not at all bothered by the interruption. "When you have children of your own some day," she said, "you'll understand."

And with that, she held out her hand to me. I climbed into her lap, enjoying the smell of her perfume and the warmth of her hands in mine. It was a peace-filled moment. Indeed, a grace-filled moment. That evening, my mother taught me the Lord's Prayer. She said the words slowly, trying to implant their meaning. Although I repeated the words, their meaning eluded me.

Twenty-five years later, I stand at my mother's bed filled with a tormented gnawing in the pit of my stomach. I am losing her and am unable to let her go.

A priest enters her room and whispers something in her ear. Even though she is unconscious, this man has the compassion to speak only to her. Turning to all of us assembled in the room, Father asks us to join hands and recite the Lord's Prayer.

I recall the evening when she taught me this prayer. And now, instead of the smell of perfume, I only smell the cancer. As I take her hand in mine, there is no warmth—only moisture as the fluid in her body can only escape through the pores of her skin. Tears sting my eyes and a silent sob closes my throat. And so we begin.

Our Father who art in heaven, hallowed be Your name . . . Miraculously, though unconscious, my mother begins to mouth the words. And we say the words slowly, so she can keep up with us.

Thy kingdom come, Thy will be done . . . For the first time, I actually hear each word.

Forgive us our trespasses, as we forgive those who trespass against us . . . It is a prayer that teaches acceptance, trust, forgiveness. It is a lesson in living. It is the life my mother led.

And lead us not into temptation, but deliver us from evil . . . In her last prayer, my mother taught us all once more.

For the kingdom, the power, and glory are Yours now and forever. And just as I did those many years ago, I feel peace and warmth. Only this time, it is our Lord's arms embracing me. The time has come for my mother to rest with Him. And now, I can let her go.

Dear Lord, grant me the grace always to accept Your will.

—**Kate Paffett**

W h e n   L o v e d   O n e s Go Home

When God removes a loved one's face,
We know He has a greater place
   For that dear one to fill—
A place where there is rest from care,
A place that sorrow cannot share,
   Nor thoughts of pain and ill.

Then God will send His love and care
To ease the burdens we now bear,
   The loneliness we feel—
And in His own good time and way
His loving presence every day
   Will all our sorrows heal.

—**Merna B. Shank**

HER HAND
IN HIS

Yet I am always with you;
you hold me by my right hand.
You guide me with your counsel,
and afterward you will take me into glory.
—Psalm 73:23–24 NIV

I had wanted to be there. I had planned to be there, sitting at the nursing home bedside of my ninety-year-old mother as she drew her last breaths. I needed to be there, I thought. I needed to hold her hand, to help her, as it were, through her final moments of earthly life.

I had wanted to be there, but I was not. I had sat at her bedside until late the night before. I had held her very warm hands in mine and had watched her thinning but familiar face, her eyes closed, her lips parted.

I had watched her turn her head, oh, so weakly, from one side of her pillow to the other. I had listened to her shallow breathing, had spooned drops of water into her dry mouth, and then had held her very warm hands again. I had prayed that God would take her soon to glory.

Yes, soon. But not until I had returned the next morning

to resume my bedside vigil, to resume holding her hands and gently squeezing them to let her know that she would not walk through her final moments alone.

Alone? Oh, no. Someone much closer to her than I was holding my mother's hand when she passed into glory in the wee hours of that next morning. The familiar hand of her precious Lord held her hand in His.

She knew Him well. She was more than just acquainted with His words. She had cherished His words. From childhood on she had hid many of His words deep within her from where they would spring up and be shared with others, especially with her children.

Through her long years of widowhood, she was comforted by and comforted others with His words of promise.

Even from her nursing home bed, her eyes dimmed and her voice trembling, she often had recited the familiar words she loved so well: "The Lord is my shepherd, I shall not want . . ." She loved to talk about the Lord's goodness to her and fold her hands in prayer.

And now, in the quiet hours of that early morning, her precious Lord took her hands in His and led her to be with Him in glory.

When my phone rang that morning with the news of my mother's death, I was momentarily saddened that I had not been at her side, holding her hand as she breathed her last. My sadness, however, soon turned to joy for I knew that He would have arranged for me to have been there had it been important for me to do so. Instead, He alone was there

. . . and I thanked Him for holding my mother's hand as she passed from death to life.

Precious Lord, thank You for Your promise to hold me by my hand. Let others see my joy in knowing that You are holding me. And when my life on earth is ending, take my hand and lead me into glory. In Jesus' name.

—**Ruth Rodewald**

$\mathcal{E}$

THROUGH THE VALLEY

OF THE SHADOW

Fear not, for I am with you. . . . I am holding you by
your right hand—I, the Lord your God—and I say to
you, Don't be afraid; I am here to help you.
—Isaiah 41:10, 13 TLB

Lord, please don't let her die alone," I pleaded.

For two weeks Mom was at what the doctor called "the window of death." I stayed by her bedside as many hours as I possibly could. When I went home each night, it was with the sinking feeling that she might not make it until morning. I knew I couldn't go with her through that dark valley, but I longed to be with her until the end. Somehow I hoped just being with her would make it easier and less frightening.

But what of my own fear? I wondered. I had never been with anyone when they died. *What if she starts gasping for breath or goes into convulsions? Can I handle it? Can I really be any help to her?*

And yet I continued to pray that the Lord would allow me to be with her. Maybe I saw it as a way to make up for all the times when I felt I hadn't been there for her. My need, perhaps, was as great as hers.

When she slipped into a coma, I despaired. Why had I waited so long, too long to say the things that needed to be said? I told her I loved her. I prayed with her. I read her promises from the Bible. In the hope that people in a coma really could hear, I kept talking, kept praying, kept reading her Scripture.

Tuesday morning my "to-do" list was especially long. I tried pushing aside the growing sense of urgency I felt to go to the hospital. *I can't spend all my time there*, I told myself. *Besides, it's not even visiting hours yet.* But unable to concentrate, I finally decided I might as well be at the hospital.

As I walked down the hospital corridor, I panicked. What if I was too late? I entered her room. Thank God, she was still breathing. She was still in a coma. Her body appeared even more emaciated than the day before, but it was her mind that really concerned me. Listening to her roommate rave, I knew I didn't want my mother to have to live the rest of her life tied in a chair and beating on herself.

"It's okay for you to go home with Jesus," I told her. "I'll miss you but you need to go with Him."

The expression on her face changed. There was a peace, a joy. I knew Jesus had entered the room. Mom's roommate abruptly stopped chattering. I wondered if she sensed His presence too.

My mother had entered the valley of the shadow, but it no longer seemed dark and frightening. Jesus was with her.

From the radiant expression on her face, I knew she had seen Him. Then, to my surprise, she slowly began to open her eyes. First one eye and then the other. She didn't speak, but she looked at me intently as I held her hand and stroked her cheek.

"Jesus has a special place prepared for you," I said. "He's going to welcome you home and give you a new mind and a new body."

I prayed with her. I quoted the Twenty-third Psalm from memory as best I could. I told her again that I loved her. I told her that I would miss her, that I needed her to cheer me on from the grandstands of heaven. Finally, there was nothing left to say or to pray.

"Jesus is going to take your hand from mine," I said as I kissed her one last time. "He's going to lead you through a beautiful valley. On the other side your loved ones will be waiting for you."

She looked at me as if torn between wanting to stay with me and wanting to go with Him. Then she closed her eyes, took one more breath, and stepped into eternity with Jesus. I wept, but my tears were tears of joy and relief. Gently and lovingly Jesus had taken her hand in His. My mother had not walked through the valley of the shadow alone. Jesus had been with her—and me.

—**Marlene Bagnull**

Life Cycle

Ashes to ashes
Some people say,
But womb to womb
Touches me this day.

I've seen my mother
Dwarfed by the bed,
Knees up, crossed arms
Waiting to be led

Through the womb
Of love and light
Into the bosom
Of our Lord, Christ.

—Patricia Walworth Wood

MEET OUR

CONTRIBUTORS

CANDY ABBOTT is Executive Secretary at Delaware Tech in Georgetown, Delaware. She and her husband, Drew, have three children and four grandchildren. A watercolor artist, calligrapher, and author of *Feelings— Prayers for Women in a Wacky World*, her hobbies are known as "Candy's Creations." Candy is also the author of *Mourning Breakers—A Daughter's Reflections of Her Mom's Homegoing*.

CHARLOTTE ADELSPERGER is a wife, mother, and third grade teacher at an independent school in Kansas City, Missouri. She is also a freelance writer, speaker, and writers' conference workshop leader. Charlotte and her husband, Bob, and their two grown children, Karen and John, enjoy marvelous memories of hiking in the Rockies in Colorado. "We are a very close family," she says.

EILEEN ANDERSON of Minnesota has been married for twenty-seven years and has two grown children. Her first published article, "A Child Without a Face," appeared in the January 1994 issue of *Guideposts* and resulted in a three-hour interview, part of which will be aired on television in a series of "stories of hope."

ELEANOR P. ANDERSON grew up in western New York state. With her pastor-husband, she has lived in several states in the east. They have three daughters, one of whom died as a teenager. Eileen has taught school, mostly kindergarten and first grade, and has written for publication since the 1950s.

COLEEN FRYE BARBER was born and raised in southern Iowa. She moved to Colorado's Rocky Mountains in 1965. She has five grown children and six grandchildren. Her work with puppets since childhood has resulted in a family ministry, the Fuzzy Folk. Coleen also enjoys ministering in musicals and solo concerts. For over three years she has written a weekly children's devotional column for her local newspaper.

VENUS E. BARDANOUVE is a retired speech pathologist and audiologist. She has three grown children and is a great-grandmother. Venus was a single mother for eleven years. She and her second husband have been married for over twenty-five years. He is a rancher and the second longest legislator in Montana's history.

KATHRYN E. BISBEE lives in Florida with her husband and two zany cats. This California native has lived almost everywhere in between as the wife of a retired Air Force serviceman. "Let there be light" (Gen. 1:3 NKJV) is the foundational thrust of her creative work in stained glass, photography, music, and writing.

DELORES ELAINE BIUS has been writing for twenty-three years and is the author of over 1,600 articles. She is an instructor for Christian Writers' Institute based in Lake Mary, Florida. Delores gives seminars at writers' conferences and libraries. She also speaks to women's groups at retreats and banquets. She lives in the midwest.

CAROLYN BOLZ is a thirty-four-year-old public school teacher in southern California. The majority of the students in her kindergarten class are from Mexico and speak only Spanish. Carolyn has a degree in Spanish and speaks it almost fluently. Her hobbies are playing the piano and reading novels. She also enjoys writing.

ROSEMARY BROWNE is seventy-one years old. She spent thirty years in the pastoral ministry with her husband of forty-three years who is now with the Lord. Rosemary's hobbies include writing, piano and organ, sewing, and floral arranging. All her life some of her best friends have been elderly. She says, "God seems to give me one at a time to whom I can be a care-taking friend." Rosemary lives in Illinois.

GEORGIA E. BURKETT and her husband, Dewey, had six children that in turn produced sixteen grandchildren and a present count of eleven great-grandchildren. Dewey is now with the Lord, as is her mother. Georgie has been a born-again Christian and active member of her church for fifty-eight years. She lives in the Harrisburg area and started writing professionally at the age of sixty-four.

MARIE BUTLER is a freelance photojournalist from Kansas City, Missouri who has had hundreds of articles and photos published in secular and Christian magazines. She has written two books: *Ron's Story* and its sequel, *The Wedging*. Marie has been on the staff of many grief groups and writers' conferences since 1978.

JOHN B. CALSIN, JR. is a full-time freelance writer

who still works temporary jobs periodically to get out from behind the desk and to keep up with what's happening in the world. He enjoys sailing, railroad train vacations, reading, and gardening in small yards. He lives near Philadelphia.

ELISE CHASE, a librarian, lives in Northampton, Massachusetts where she has been active in volunteer work with the homeless through the ministries of her local church community. For ten years she served as *Library Journal's* "Inspirational Reading" columnist. She has compiled a bibliography of Christian self-help books entitled *Healing Faith*, and is the author of *A Home to Dwell In: One Woman's Journey Beyond Divorce.*

ANNE CLACK is a wife, mother, and grandmother from Florida. She says, "Our family of five children had a habit of bringing or sending young people to live with us. I can count nineteen or so youngsters who lived with us for more than a month. Some for years. We were unofficial foster parents." Anne writes book reviews and testimonies.

BERT CLOMPUS began writing while in grade school but, at sixty, he really began writing after reading the Bible and becoming a true believer. He started getting published after attending the St. Davids Christian Writers' Conference near his home in Pennsylvania. His stories have appeared in *Guideposts, Christian Herald,* and *The Messenger of St. Anthony.*

JOAN CORRIE and her husband work together in his accounting office which is located next to their home on a small farm in Illinois. Eleven llamas share the acreage with them. Joan enjoys photography, reading, sewing, and Bible studies. All of this, plus life with children and grandchildren, give her ample material for writing meditations.

ELAINE CUNNINGHAM is a program assistant for the Columbia River Area Agency on Aging in Wenatchee, Washington. She is married to a minister. They have a daughter who is a teacher and a son who is a missionary. She has recently coauthored a book with her son entitled *Madagascar: The Island at the End of the World.* She has authored four other books and numerous stories and articles.

MARY LYNN DAVIS was a full-time mother for ten years. She helped her husband start a business and now teaches English at Phillips Junior College in Jackson, Mississippi. Mary Lynn's main interests are studying the Bible, reading, and visiting with family and friends. Her son, John, is a physician in his first year of a neurosurgery residency. Her daughter, Anne, is a college senior majoring in interior design.

MARY ANN L. DIORIO is a wife, mother, freelance writer, musician, artist, and businesswoman. She has her doctorate in French and comparative literature. Mary Ann is the head writer for a television program for teens as well as the author of three books and numerous articles and short stories. She and her husband, Dominic, a physician, have two daughters, Lia Cristina, age 20, and Gina Luciana, age 16, and live in New Jersey.

DAVID DODGE is one of eleven children born to missionary parents. His wife is one of ten children. She was born and raised on a Texas sheep and goat ranch. They have three children. Their firstborn drowned when he was seventeen. David has developed a county jail ministry. He publishes *The Prison Journal* for prisoners around the nation.

JUDITH DEEM DUPREE is a poet, teacher, and the author of *Going Home*. She also writes fiction, music, and children's literature and has taught adult Christian education and poetry workshops. She and her husband live in a small mountain village in southern California. They have three grown children.

JUNE EATON took early retirement after twenty-three years as a classroom teacher to work for Christian Life Missions where she served for seven years as director of the Christian Writers' Institute. Now retired with her husband, Fred, she says, "I am just getting started in a free-lance writing ministry. Together we are heavily into the grandparenting business." They live near Chicago.

BEVERLY ELIASON teaches fourth and fifth grade Sunday school and is active in prison ministry. She is married with five children and three grandchildren and lives near Philadelphia. She is presently taking courses through the Moody Correspondence School of Bible Study and regularly writes for Christian publications.

ELAINE M. ENGLERT came to know the Lord while in high school. Shortly after, she met her husband, Mark. She taught preschool and then "retired" to begin nursery school with their three children. For the first time in thirteen years, she is without preschoolers. Elaine lives in New York and keeps busy with church and school activities, water jogging, crafts, and sewing.

LORETTA K. EVANS is an artist, writer, medical assistant, and pastor's wife. She and her husband have five children—four sons and one daughter. All are Christians and married to Christians! They have six grandchildren with one on the way. Her husband is presently serving their fourth church in Massachusetts.

MARY FENDER has raised five children and worked for various government agencies in southern Maryland. In 1984 she served as a short-term assistant secretary to the Director of the Senegal, Gambia, and Guinea-Bissau Branch of Wycliffe Bible Translators. Mary enjoys watercolor painting and is pursuing the art of being a loving and caring mother and grandmother.

VICKIE FERGUSON lives in Denver but was born and raised in North Carolina. She has taught English, history, and journalism in secondary schools. Career moves by her husband have taken her to St. Louis, Los Angeles, and to Denver a second time. As a mother of three, she returned to college and earned a masters in communication. She readily acknowledges God's power to lead us where He would have us go.

SHIRLEY FOLWARSKI is a wife, mother, homemaker, and freelance writer from Oklahoma. She and her husband, Frank, have five children and two-plus grandchildren. Shirley has been a short-term missionary nurse to Eastern Europe, Africa, South America, and the Philippines. She has recently had a missions story accepted by *Guideposts*.

SANDRA FORSTER is an avid horse enthusiast and at the present time is working with the Pennsylvania Equine Council in compiling an Equine Industry Directory. She and her husband celebrated their thirtieth wedding anniversary last year. They have four children and two grandchildren. Her mother-in-law lives in a mobile home in their yard. Sandra has taught Sunday school and worked with youth groups.

JUNE GILBAUGH was a high school English teacher for fifteen years until back surgery took her from the classroom. Although interested in writing all her life, she did not have much time to devote to it until she became disabled. Since then her writing has won more than fifty awards. Her husband, Ward, is an accomplished organist and pianist. Together they fulfill at least fifty engagements a year to sing, play, and read June's poetry. They reside in Ohio.

CATHY JEAN GOHLKE has written human interest, news, and feature articles for local newspapers. She volunteers in the Book Buddy Program of the public library, developing friendships and sharing books with nursing home patients. Cathy enjoys working with elementary grade children in a school library program, writing, reading, gardening, photography, and creative activities with her children. She and her husband, Dan, have a daughter and son and make their home in Elkton, Maryland.

ANNE H. GROSS is a freelance writer who has lived most of her life near Pittsburgh. She has been married for forty-seven years to a minister who is also a psychologist. She is active in church work and volunteer jobs, currently tutoring fifth graders in a Christian setting. She has enjoyed writing since childhood. Anne and her husband have three children and three grandchildren.

JOSIE HALBERT was born in New Orleans and has lived in the metropolitan area all her life. She is a secretary for one of the local oil companies. Her spare time is filled with writing, church activities, caring for her elderly father, and membership in their local Christian Coalition. Josie and her husband live in his childhood home with their cats, Jasper and Naomi, and Pekoe, an amazing tap dancing cockatiel.

GRACE HAN is the 3–11 nurse supervisor in a suburban Philadelphia nursing home. Her hobbies include reading, gardening, music, exploring new places, and people watching. Literacy work with children and teaching prison inmates how to make better decisions are important volunteer efforts. Grace writes poetry and edits her church newsletter. She has been a believer and follower of Jesus Christ since childhood.

JAMES HANAK is the founder and director of American Family Ministries. He works with local churches to develop small group ministries that will strengthen the family unit. He received his doctorate in Discipleship and Evangelism and specializes in finding workable solutions to complex social issues. He recently began hosting the cable TV talk show *Studio 7* which reaches the Philadelphia main line.

RUTH HARRISON is the great-granddaughter of a missionary and granddaughter of a minister. She was born in the West Indies, grew up in New York City, and taught French and English in the middle and senior high schools of her small Pennsylvania town. She is an elder in her church, mother of two grown daughters, and married to

Bob, a retired bank marketer with whom she writes scripts and plans cultural exchanges for young people. Together they enjoy travel, fine arts, theater, good friends, and helping Bob's ninety-two-year-old mother to maintain her independent way of life.

HELEN HEAVIRLAND enjoys nature, hiking, cross-country skiing, reading, singing, writing music, and enough other subjects and activities that she'll be busy way into eternity. She has been published in more than twenty magazines. She lives with her husband near Milton-Freewater, Oregon.

ETHEL HERR is a freelance writer, writing instructor, historian, and conference speaker from California. She enjoys sewing, cooking, traveling, and playing with her three grandchildren. She and her husband cared for their mothers and Ethel's grandmother in their home for fourteen years. Both of Ethel's grandmothers lived past one hundred years.

MARY HERRON is married to a United Methodist minister and finds many areas in which to serve. She has her lay speaker's certificate and is also a certified nurse's assistant doing mostly home nursing of the elderly. Mary has taught ceramics. She designed her daughter's clothes when she was at home. She resides in northeastern Pennsylvania.

BARBARA HIBSCHMAN team teaches at marriage retreats with her husband, Jim, who is pastor of Alliance Bible Church in Warren, New Jersey. They are former missionaries to the Philippines. Barbara began writing ten years ago and now is the author of eight books and over two hundred articles and poems. She is a popular speaker at women's groups and Christian education, missions, and writers conferences. Barbara was especially close to her father since he raised her as a single parent from the time she was two years old.

ALETHA HINTHORN is the editor of *Women Alive!* and founder of Women Alive, a nondenominational organization which encourages women teaching women. She has taught home Bible studies for many years and written one book, *They Pleased God Through Faith.* She has also written Sunday school materials, articles, and Bible studies. Aletha and her husband, Daniel, a medical doctor, live in Kansas. They have two children.

PHOEBE BELL HONIG is the wife of a retired engineer and mother of three grown sons. "Bing" calls writing her most fulfilling activity. She also enjoys sketching, creative cooking, swimming, walking, berry picking, games, travel, leading adult study groups, and sporadically playing the piano when she can spare time from her second-most-favorite activity, reading. Bing lives in Massachusetts.

MARSHA OWENS HOOD is an American Baptist poet and reading specialist who has taught reading and language arts for the past twenty-four years in grades K–12. She lives in Carnegie, Pennsylvania, with her husband, Dan, and their children, Lisa and Dusty.

CORA SCOTT HOWELL cared for her father until he died of emphysema. She frequently visits people in personal care homes. Freelance writing and spending time with four children and two grandchildren are her hobbies. She and her husband live near Apollo, Pennsylvania.

JANET MILANO IHLE, a full-time wife and mother, lives with her husband, Bill, in Caro, Michigan. Their daughters, Trina and Lita, both attend college. Janet is on the board of Tuscola County Big Brothers/Big Sisters and is active in her church. She is also the editor of *Thumbprints*, the newsletter of the Thumb Area Writer's Club. Janet and her family cared for her mother in their home for several months during her last year.

LYN JACKSON and her husband live in Colorado and have a son and a married daughter. All of them, including their son-in-law, are involved in some phase of the publishing business. Lyn is active in the women's ministry program of her church. She writes a weekly column, feature articles for a suburban newspaper, and publicity and advertising copy for a denominational publishing house and chain of grocery stores. She also writes children's fiction, devotionals, and greeting cards. In "Please, Lord, Not Today!" Lyn wrote about an experience her sister, Twyla Wilson, had in caring for their mother.

ALYCE MITCHEM JENKINS lives in Warren, New Jersey with her husband, Dr. Reese V. Jenkins, Director of the Edison Papers Project at Rutgers University. The mother of two adult children, Alyce writes and speaks about adoption. She has taught English and social studies in Wisconsin, Illinois, Ohio, and New Jersey and has written for numerous Christian and secular publications.

HELEN KAMMERDIENER lives in the small village of Putneyville nestled in a western Pennsylvania valley.

She has been an elementary teacher for thirty years. When her parents needed more support, she purchased a mobile home and placed it beside her parents' home. Her daily schedule usually includes a trip to Clarview's Nursing and Rehab Center to help her father eat supper. Writing, she says, is a stress reliever.

JUDY EBLE KIEL says "my profession is wife and mother! I delivered my children by natural childbirth in the late sixties when nobody was doing it. My role as wife and mother is surely God's special gift to me." Judy also enjoys teaching a Bible class and singing in her church choir. She has a cottage business, Poems with Personality, and has written human interest articles for three southern Indiana newspapers.

NAN McKENZIE KOSOWAN lives in Canada and learned the power of sharing words of the heart through a grade seven composition. She found her husband and a career on the University of Toronto newspaper. She has been a small town reporter, columnist, women's editor, and staff writer for World Vision of Canada. Nan gave control of her life to Jesus when her two children were tiny. She has counseled troubled Christian women for thirty years.

BETTY KOSSICK has been freelance writing for twenty-three years for both the religious and secular press. She is a native Ohioan but with her husband has lived in three states. He has just recently retired, and they have moved to Michigan. They are the parents of two and the grandparents of five. Betty is active in her church, currently serving on the elder team. Her personal philosophy is "Others."

FAYE LANDRUM is a sixty-five-year-old grandmother, a retired nurse, and a freelance writer. Her work has been published in over seventy-five adult publications. She has coauthored a series of take-home Sunday school pamphlets for primary-age children as well as two books, *Midweek Messages* and *86 Crafts from Plastic Castoffs*. Faye lives in Ohio.

SHERRI LANGTON is assistant editor of *Bible Advocate* magazine. Sherri is also a freelance writer of articles and poetry and the publisher of Godsend greeting cards. She lives in Colorado and is active in the music ministry of her church.

KAREN GRONVALL LARSON says, "I love Jesus and seek to serve Him, especially through writing and prayer." She is married with two sons, two daughters-in-law, and two grandchildren. Karen sang in the church choir, substituted as secretary in the church office, and volunteered at a Dorothy Day House until her recent move to another Minnesota town.

CATHERINE LAWTON lives in northern California with her husband, Larry, and their two teenagers. They are active in their local church as Sunday school teachers and musicians. Cathy volunteers for several community organizations and is a licensed minister in the Church of the Nazarene. Her articles and poems have appeared in many religious periodicals. Cathy says that reading, walking, gardening, piano playing, prayer, and friends "fill my soul needs. I want to give my all to God for all He's given to me."

MARCIA KRUGH LEASER is a wife and mother with two grown children. She also is a Christian clown. She performs at nursing homes and hospitals with her daughters and a friend who have a puppet ministry. Marcia has been writing for twenty years and has 365 articles and poems in print. She is also a songwriter—both words and music. Her leisure time is spent reading or walking in the woods behind her Ohio home.

CELIA LEHMAN is a retired teacher and freelance writer who lives in Ohio. She has been a community correspondent for *The Wooster Daily Record* and has also authored three books. Celia taught overseas for two years and then returned home to marry a widower who had four teenage children. It was during this time that she helped care for her ailing mother.

CAROL STEVENS LEONARD enjoys writing devotionals from children's chatterings that were collected over the years. She also makes greeting cards, writes human interest articles and poems, and is pursuing photography to enhance her writing. She lives in Toledo, Ohio.

ELLEN LETHBRIDGE is a veteran youth worker and currently a full-time mom living in New Hampshire. Because family relationships are her high priority, she has chosen to home-school her children. Although her focus is on the home front, Ellen continues to do volunteer work. Her desire is to publish inspirational and resource materials which nurture critical thinking skills. Pencil sketches, cross-stitch, singing, and the dream of sewing a quilt are creative outlets.

MARTHA J. VAN DER LINDEN was born and raised in the South. She married her college sweetheart; they had three children, Donna, Scott, and Brooke, who died in 1988. Martha has been a Sunday school teacher for eighteen years and a trained caregiver in the Stephen Ministry for eight years. She walks three miles daily at dawn. She also enjoys tennis, bridge, skiing, collecting clowns, and writing. She is a member of the Capital Speaker's Club and lives in Maryland.

SANDRA ALLEN LOVELACE is a forty-five-year-old Massachusetts woman celebrating her twenty-fifth year of marriage. She has two daughters, ages eleven and fifteen. With her husband she served on the staff of L'Abri Fellowship in Switzerland. Sandra and her husband direct Lifework Forum, a speaker's bureau providing fresh insights into age-old questions and contemporary issues. She has been writing for ten years.

ARETTA LOVING and her husband are Wycliffe missionaries who have just recently returned to Papua, New Guinea after a busy six-month furlough in the states. Aretta is a proud mom and grandmom. She has written many interesting stories about their ministry in Kenya (and earlier ministry in Papua, New Guinea) that have been printed in various Christian periodicals.

HELEN LUECKE lives with her husband, Richard, in the Texas panhandle city of Amarillo. They have two grown sons, a lovely daughter-in-law, and one grandson. Helen works as a directory assistance operator for South-western Bell Telephone Company. She is a published writer who aspires to write devotionals, short stories, and novels for the glory of the Lord.

BETTIE MacMORRAN is a "Hoosier" born in Indiana but "transplanted" at six months to Kansas. The family moved back to Indiana when she was twelve. Consequently the prairies and wheat fields of Kansas vie for first place in her heart with the rolling hills of southern Indiana. She and her husband have three sons, one daughter, and eight grandchildren. Last year they retired and moved from the family home into a cottage they built. They are enjoying the more simple life. Bettie says, "I love keeping house in a dollhouse!"

TARA MARTIN is a freelance writer, newspaper columnist, and speaker who has published over 400 newspaper columns, editorials, and feature stories. Tara and her husband have two adult sons and reside in Valparaiso, Indiana.

MARY MARVIN and her husband live in New York and have three married sons and two grandchildren. In addition to helping her brother and sisters care for her mother, she does the preschool story hour and summer reading club in a local library. Mary enjoys writing, crafts, gardening, country walks, and reading. She plays the trombone in a music group that gives concerts in the park and programs for nursing homes.

EDNA MAST is a retired teacher and former editor who has been writing since serving on her high school paper staff. She enjoys her family, church activities, reading, and homemaking. She and Alvin, her husband of fifty-six years, have five children, eleven grandchildren, and three great-grandchildren. They are presently waiting for the pipes to thaw so that the plumbers can move ahead on the apartment that is being remodeled for them in their daughter's Pennsylvania farmhouse.

MARGARET I. MILLER and her husband, Eugene, are living at the Rockhill Mennonite Community in southeastern Pennsylvania. Last year they celebrated his eighty-fifth birthday with a surprise party. Margaret also had a public speaking engagement that week and a "business lunch" with another writer. Margaret writes out of her experiences in nursing. After graduating from Lankenau Hospital's School of Nursing she worked as a pediatric instructor at the Children's Hospital of the Mary Drexel Home.

EVELYN MINSHULL is the author of seventeen published books and hundreds of short stories, poems, plays, and articles. A teacher in public schools for twenty-five-plus years, she currently conducts writing workshops at writers' conferences, in schools, and at elder-hostels. She and her husband, Fred, live near Pittsburgh and have three grown children and a granddaughter.

DIANE MITCHELL and her husband of twenty-eight years have three biological children and an adopted daughter with special needs (Down's syndrome). Diane is the coordinator of a program for retarded citizens in Onedia, New York and also serves as the facilitator of a support group for parents of handicapped children. Diane has taught many women's Bible study groups and spoken at a number of luncheons and meetings for Christian women.

RUTH E. MONTGOMERY has been a radio speaker, rural schoolteacher, and a missionary housewife. She and her husband have four married children. Ruth has written more than 125 published pieces. She also speaks at writers' conferences and is the founder and past president of the Learners Christian Writing Club in Kansas.

MARY BETH NELSON is a retired elementary teacher with four grown children, nine grandchildren, and a wonderful husband. Her favorite volunteer work in their small community of Clarendon, Texas, is a music therapy class which she has been conducting each Monday afternoon at the Clarendon Nursing Home for the past nine years. Mary Beth is also interested in gardening and music.

GWEN NORTHCUTT is a seventy-two-year-old retiree who celebrated her fiftieth wedding anniversary last year. She and her husband have two married children. She has been writing all of her life, mostly gratis. A Christian drug abuse ministry and her church are just two of the organizations that have benefited from her gift with words. She makes her home in Maryland.

JEAN M. OLSEN retired in 1985 after thirty-two years of service with Africa Inland Mission. She and her husband have two grown daughters and three grandchildren. Since 1986 she has been a caregiver for an Alzheimer's patient, a nursery school music teacher, and at present, church secretary. She teaches five piano pupils. Jean has a growing writing ministry and resides in New Jersey.

KAREN L. ONESTI is an ordained minister in the United Methodist Church. She pastors two congregations in southern New Jersey and is also adjunct professor of Greek Language and Exegesis at Eastern Baptist Theological Seminary in Philadelphia. Her research on Greek fragments has been published in Jerusalem. She and her husband, Frank, have two children. Karen is a bibliophile and enjoys calligraphy.

KATE PAFFETT is very active working with the youth in her parish. She coordinated a trip to see the pope when he was in Colorado last summer. Kate has five children, a great sense of humor, and lots of energy. She lives near Philadelphia.

FLORENCE E. PARKES accepted Christ as her Savior when she was eight years old. Her husband is a retired pastor. They have three children—a daughter who teaches in a Christian school, another daughter who is a pastor's wife, and a son who is a pastor. They have eight grandchildren—four of each. Florence enjoys playing piano and helping with programs at church. Her writing has been published in a number of Christian periodicals. She lives in Maryland.

FRANCES GREGORY PASCH has had numerous poems and articles published. She also enjoys journaling and letter writing. Frances is president of her local Christian Writers' Fellowship and enjoys encouraging new writers. She and her husband, Jim, have five grown sons and reside in North Plainfield, New Jersey.

MARGARET PRIMROSE was a Nebraska farm girl who always liked to write. After about twenty years of teaching in the states and South America, she joined the staff of *Indian Life* at the America Indian Mission in South Dakota. Five years later she went to the Nazarene Publishing House where she has been the office editor of *Come Ye Apart* for most of her sixteen years in Kansas City.

BOB RANDALL has been a pastor for thirty-eight years. He and his wife, Shirley, have lived in western Pennsylvania most of their lives. In the 70s, he worked as an editor at Whitaker House. Bob is pursuing several writing and editing projects including a full-length book on the kingdom of God. He loves teaching, painting, drama, and gardening.

LOIS REESE and her first husband moved to Colorado in 1972 with their two children to manage their own health food store. He passed away in 1978 after a long illness. Lois moved with her children to Utah where she married her second husband, Ron. Between them they have six children and thirteen grandchildren who Lois says are "our greatest teachers." Her hobbies are hiking, directing music, photography, and knitting. She is also a composer.

LaVEL REICHLE is married and the mother of two grown daughters. She teaches Sunday school and currently coordinates Children's Church. She has directed choirs for children, youth, and adults in church and as an outreach. She has had numerous inspirational articles and stories published. LaVel enjoys one-on-one prayer counseling, reading, Bible study, and homemaking. She makes her home in Missouri.

FAYE ROBERTS and her husband, Tom, live in Colorado and have four children ranging in age from seven to twenty. She had a career in banking for thirteen years, recently switching to part-time. Her writing has appeared in leading Christian magazines. She was selected for the 1988 *Guideposts* Writers' Workshop. Faye's hobbies include horseback riding, reading, collecting quotations, gardening, and growing roses.

BETTY BENSON ROBERTSON is an author, speaker, writing/marketing consultant, editor, and publisher. Her ten books include *T*L*C for Aging Parents*. She is also the editorial director for Parent Care Publications (see p. 377) and conducts Parent Care Seminars around the country. Betty and her husband live in Virginia where he pastors Roanoke First Church of the Nazarene. They have two grown children who have promised to care for them, as needed, in their old age!

RUTH RODEWALD and her retired minister-husband live in Concordia, Missouri. They have five children and ten grandchildren. Ruth spent most of her married years as a full-time homemaker. Ten years ago she began working at the newspaper office in her small town. Self-taught in journalism skills, she eventually became the news and features writer for the paper. She retired from that job last year and currently volunteers her time to write publicity for a private high school in Concordia.

MARY HARWELL SAYLER has been writing for children and adults for over twenty years. She's had several books published and hundreds of short pieces in a variety of religious publications. Since 1982 she has worked with Christian writers and now instructs through The Word Center in DeLand, Florida.

ALICE EVERETT SCHOCK and her husband have two grown children, a daughter-in-law, and an eighteen-month granddaughter. As a registered nurse caring for senior citizens, Alice has countless opportunities to interact with patients and their families. One of her chosen verses is Proverbs 12:25 (NIV): "An anxious heart weighs a man down, but a kind word cheers him up." Her interests include traveling to new places, reading humorous stories, classical music, and meeting people from other countries. She lives in Colorado.

KATHY SCOTT has been freelance writing since 1977. She is a news correspondent for Lancaster, Pennsylvania newspapers and has had 300 articles in other publications. She is the editor of *Calvary Tidings* published by her church. She also teaches junior Sunday school. Kathy is past president of the Lancaster County chapter of Pennsylvania Farm Women and an alumni council member of Lancaster Bible College.

MERNA B. SHANK lives with her adult daughter and son in Harrisonburg, Virginia where she is also secretary at Christian Light Publications, the organization founded by her late husband, Sanford. As a pastor's wife and secretary, Merna had limited time for hobbies through the years, but she did find some time for crocheting and reading in addition to writing. She has published numerous poems, short articles, and meditations plus two booklets of verse for children and the greeting booklet, *My Soul's Delights* (see p. 378).

JESSICA SHAVER lives in California and freelances for Christian magazines and newspapers. She writes on subjects as varied as abortion, evolution, child abuse, archaeology, nuclear weapons, academic freedom, tax evasion, and sailing. *Gianna*, her book about a girl who survived her mother's abortion, was published last fall by Focus on the Family. She writes a poetry column for *The Christian Communicator*. Jessica and her husband, Rick, have two children in college.

FLORA M. SMITH has held many different jobs over the sixty years of her life but says the most important and satisfying have been wife and mother. Now in retirement she feels God's gentle nudge toward the typewriter. She has always loved to write but has never been published. Flora and her husband recently moved to North Carolina after having lived in the northeast and midwest. They are building a home in the woods and looking forward to discovering what God has planned for this part of their lives. Faith and family are her highest priorities.

SARA L. SMITH is a "forty-something" wife, mother, daughter, employee, freelance writer, and member of the "sandwich generation." Her husband is a career civil servant and their five children (ages ten to twenty) all live at home. Besides ministering to her family, Sara works part-time in a school cafeteria and writes whenever she can. In her spare time she enjoys baking, reading, and playing with her cats.

PATRICIA SOUDER and her husband, David, have three children and live in northeastern Pennsylvania. Patti works part-time as a nurse. She is a published writer and a speaker/soloist for women's retreats, mother-daughter banquets, and Christian Women's Clubs. She teaches Sunday school, directs the choir, and writes scripts for musicals and dramas. Patti is also the assistant director of the Montrose Bible Conference Christian Writers' Conference.

BETTY C. STEVENS loves to write devotions which she believes is an outgrowth of living with or near older loved ones. Her husband's parents lived across the street from them, and her husband's aunt and uncle and a maiden aunt lived next door. Betty's mother lived with them. She says, "I had much to learn, and God taught me." Her daughter, son-in-law, and grandson now live in that house across the street in western Pennsylvania.

SHIRLEY S. STEVENS is cofounder and leader of The First Word, a Christian writers' group based in Sewickly, Pennsylvania. She is past president of the St. David's Christian Writers' Conference. Shirley is also the English coordinator at Quaker Valley High School in Leetsdale, the author of a volume of poetry (*Pronouncing What We Wish to Keep*), a poetry tutor with The Writing Academy, and a board member of The International Poetry Forum.

PEGGY STRAIN is a Pennsylvania farm wife and mother of three children. She makes cheese and churns butter. She also conducts teaching tours on the farm for nursery schools and cub scouts and teaches programs on farm life at the local elementary school. Peggy writes the weekly lesson for teaching an adult Bible study class.

NANCY TEMPLEMAN is married and has three grown children and three grandchildren. She is a former teacher. With a friend she founded the Rochester Christian Writers' Fellowship. In addition to being active in her church, she is a group leader in Community Bible Study. Gardening and quilting are her favorite pastimes.

LEAH THORNE is the pen name of a retired college professor who specialized in teaching poetry and creative writing, both in the United States and more recently in Japan. She lives with three cats in western Pennsylvania. One is named Clown, another is an aging feline, and the third is a Japanese immigrant.

MARILYN P. TURNER is an African-American who has a special desire to see more believers with her cultural heritage represented in the Christian media. Marilyn's dream is to provide writing and teaching which will encourage souls for Christ. While she prays and works toward the realization of that dream, she supports herself and her delightful nine-year-old son, Stephen, by working as a manager in the telecommunications industry. She lives in a suburb of Philadelphia.

JUNE L. VARNUM is a widow with two married sons and six grandchildren. She is her eighty-nine-year-old mother's primary caregiver. Reading, walking, and enjoying nature are June's favorite pastimes. June teaches Sunday school and vacation Bible school, leads prayer and women's Bible study groups, occasionally speaks at women's meetings, and leads a Christian writers' critique group. She lives in Nevada.

BARBARA A. WALK is a church librarian and novice poet. She resides in western Pennsylvania with her husband, David. They share a love of choral music, gardening, reading, and relaxing with their dog, Clover. Barbara is currently studying voice and performing in Christian musical productions. Her other favorite activities include inductive Bible study, resale shopping, musical drama, nature walks, and herbal cooking.

KATHLEEN A. WALKER is married and the mother of

four grown children. A fifth child died at age fourteen. She has two granddaughters. Kathleen works full-time as a secretary in the Gerontology Department of a hospital in New Jersey. She started evening college in 1989 as a communications major and started journaling and writing poetry the year she turned fifty. It is her hope that in the second half of her personal century God will allow her to communicate His message to others through writing, speaking, or both.

CAROL WEDEVEN and her tribologist husband, Vern, live near Philadelphia and have four children ages eighteen to twenty-three. Carol enjoys being wife and mother, teaching, writing, reading, guest-authoring in schools, playing the piano and organ, singing, painting, acting, and being with children. She has published articles, poetry, curriculum, and a picture book, *The Christmas Crib That Zack Built.* She directs the St. David's Christian Writers' Conference.

GRAYCE L. WEIBLEY has had over a hundred articles published. She writes monologues for women of the Bible and presents them in costume. Besides writing, she enjoys teaching, speaking, reading, volunteer work, and all types of needle crafts. She and her husband of fifty years have two grown children and live in Asheville, North Carolina.

PATRICIA WALWORTH WOOD presents entertaining, inspirational, and educational programs to church groups, public schools, hospitals, prison groups, health care centers, and other groups. Writing is her first love. She has been published in numerous magazines. Patricia and her husband have two children and two grandchildren and live in Indiana. They have hosted high school exchange students, a Cambodian refugee, and college students from other countries.

PAULINE YOUD is married with three grown children and three granddaughters. She lives in California where she sings in the church choir and is involved with her husband in a community chorus and the reconciliation ministry of their church. She has elementary and secondary teaching credentials and currently tutors reading. Her hobby is writing. Her book, *Adopted for a Purpose,* was published by Abingdon. She has had articles and devotionals in other Christian periodicals.

CHERYL L. ZIMMERMAN works as a registered nurse in a long-term care facility and has sixteen years experience in caring for the elderly. She was born and raised in Erie, Pennsylvania. She wrote her first story in second grade and her first poetry at twelve years of age. She wrote and directed her church's Christmas program in 1993 with the fine arts team of her church. It included dance, sign, mime, and drama.

&

RECOMMENDED

READING

Armstrong, Mary Vaughn. *Caregiving for Your Loved Ones.* Elgin, IL: LifeJourney Books, a division of David C. Cook Publishing Co., 1990. Written by a caregiver who learned the importance of taking care of herself. The author's honesty will speak deeply to weary caregivers.

Bathauer, Ruth M. *Parent Care.* Ventura, CA: Regal Books, 1990. A well-written and thorough resource book loaded with practical ideas and suggestions.

Deane, Barbara. *Caring for Your Aging Parents—When Love Is Not Enough.* Colorado Springs, CO: NavPress, 1989. Written by the cofounder of Christian Caregivers, this is a comprehensive and well-documented handbook on practical as well as spiritual and relational issues.

Carol Dettoni. *Caring for Those Who Can't—Caregiving for Your Loved One—and Yourself.* Wheaton, IL: Victor Books, 1993. Although the focus of this book is not just on caring for aging parents, it will prove to be helpful and encouraging reading.

Elliot, Elisabeth. *Forget Me Not—Loving God's Aging Children.* Portland, OR: Multnomah Press, 1989. An illustrated gift book of the twelve insights the author gained as she watched the erosion of her mother's memory.

Fanning, Marilyn. *Compassionate Care, Practial Love for Your Aging Parents.* Lynwood, WA: Aglow, 1994. Spiritual sustenance for inevitable hard times and practical insights into caregiving. The author cared for both of her parents for several years. Contains a helpful up-to-date resource list.

Gibson, Dennis and Ruth. *The Sandwich Years—When Your Kids Need Friends and Your Parents Need Parenting.* Grand Rapids, MI: Baker Book House, 1991. Written with humor and insight by family counselors who have lived through the sandwich years in their own family.

Hamlin, Dr. Judy. *Caring for Your Aging Parents—6 Sensitive Studies for Women with Families in Transition.* Wheaton, IL: Victor Books, 1992. How I wish this study book with its strong scriptural base had been available while I was caring for my mother. Contains helpful leader notes, so if you do not already have a support group in your church or community, why not start one?

Horne, Jo. *A Survival Guide for Family Caregivers*. Roanoke, VA: Parent Care Publications, 1991. Helps with assessment, formulating methods, and planning for the future.

Hover, Margot. *Caring for Yourself When Caring for Others*. Mystic, CT: Twenty-Third Publications, 1993. The author weaves Scripture, personal stories, situational experiences, and prayer into a practical and uplifting guide for caregivers.

Johnson, Richard P., Ph.D. *Aging Parents—How to Understand and Help Them*. Liguori, MO: Liguori Publications, 1987. Help for building a healthy relationship with your aging parents and understanding the issues they are facing.

Riekse, Dr. Robert J. and Holstege, Dr. Henry. *The Christian Guide to Parent Care*. Wheaton, IL: Tyndale House Publishers, Inc., 1992. Helping aging parents meet their changing needs—physical, emotional, and spiritual. Includes a list of national organizations for caregivers.

Robertson, Betty. *T*L*C for Aging Parents*. Kansas City, MO: Beacon Hill Press, 1992. A well-researched and practical step-by-step how-to book with an appendix of reproducible charts and forms that will be valuable tools for busy caregivers.

Rushford, Pat. *Caring for Elderly Parents*. Grand Rapids, MI: Fleming H. Revell, 1993. Detailed information and

practical help for dealing with the many problems of
caring for aging parents.

Shank, Merna B. *My Soul's Delights—God's Comfort in
Sorrow*. Harrisonburg, VA: Christian Light Publications, 1991. Merna combined her poetry with her son's
photography to create a beautiful gift booklet.

Smick, Timothy S. and others. *Eldercare for the Christian
Family*. Dallas, TX: Word Publishing, 1990. Explores
all the dynamics of caregiving—planning, financing,
burnout, and blessing.

Temple, Todd and Green, Tracy. *52 Ways to Show Aging
Parents You Care*. Nashville, TN: Thomas Nelson Publishers, 1992. New and creative and fun ideas to
brighten your parents' days.

Subscribe to *Parent Care,* a monthly newsletter for children of aging parents, for encouraging articles from other
caregivers, helpful tips and suggestions, book reviews,
new product information, and inspiration from God's
Word. Published by Creative Christian Ministries, Box
12624, Roanoke, VA 24027. Also write for a copy of their
Idea Catalog which provides a comprehensive listing of
books, special reports, and other resources to help you care
for your aging parent.

WHAT IS

HEAVEN LIKE?

A few hours before Jesus Christ died, He hosted a dinner with His twelve disciples. At this dinner He revealed that His death was imminent. Because His disciples were in as much danger as Jesus Himself, He felt it important to tell them that death should not be feared. Rather it should be welcomed as a friend.

"Do not let your hearts be troubled. Trust in God; trust also in me. In my Father's house are many rooms; if it were not so, I would have told you. I am going there to prepare a place for you. And if I go and prepare a place for you, I will come . . . and take you to be with me that you also may be where I am." [1]

Jesus is preparing a place for all who are headed for heaven. What is that place going to be like?

Those who knew Jesus best have revealed to us what we will experience when the time comes to walk through the gates of heaven. In heaven there will be no darkness. [2] God will provide light for us to see. [3] There will be no night and there will be no need to rest, for everything we experience in heaven will be restful. [4] Ours will be lives of

379

complete joy and happiness, for there will be no tears, death, mourning, crying, or pain.[5]

Although we will be invited to sit with God at a banquet table[6] in comfortable surroundings,[7] and will be able to enjoy the food He prepares,[8] there will be no thirst[9] or hunger.[10]

We will not feel any shame, nor will we ever meet anyone who will try to deceive us.[11]

God will allow us to know more about Him than we can possibly imagine.[12] That will be possible because we will be able to talk to Jesus face-to-face,[13] and our resurrection bodies will be just like His.[14] Although we will recognize each other,[15] we will not be married as we were on earth.[16] God has designed it so our needs for intimacy will be fulfilled through our relationship with Christ Himself.[17]

In heaven, we will no longer be afraid of God,[18] nor will we quarrel with each other.[19] Along with millions of others[20] from every nation, tribe, people, and language,[21] our attention will be on praising, worshiping,[22] and serving[23] He who created us.[24] Christ will give us great responsibilities as we reign with Him,[25] as we will even act as judges over the angels of heaven.[26]

In heaven, our home will be a great city that will be modeled after the city of Jerusalem, the temple, and the garden of Eden.[27] This city will have a splendor greater than anything we can imagine.[28]

All of this will last for eternity—it will never end.[29]

It is for this reason one prominent Jew, after meeting the resurrected Jesus, said,

"We are confident, I say, and would prefer to be away from the body and at home with the Lord." [30]

The question then becomes, "How can I know that I am headed for this fantastic place?" The answer is amazingly simple. Jesus' closest disciple wrote a letter to let us know how simple it is. In it he told us,

". . . these are written that you may believe that Jesus is the Christ, the Son of God, and that by believing you may have life in his name." [31]

That letter is available to us today. It is the fourth book of the New Testament, the book of John.

—Dr. James Hanak

1. John 14:1–3 NIV
2. Rev. 22:5
3. Rev. 22:5
4. Rev. 14:13
5. Rev. 21:4
6. Rev. 19:9
7. Rev. 7:16
8. Luke 24:41–43
9. Rev. 21:6
10. Rev. 7:16
11. Rev. 21:27
12. 1 Cor. 13:12
13. 1 Cor. 13:12
14. 1 John 3:2
15. Matt. 17:3;
    Heb. 12:1
16. Matt. 22:30
17. Matt. 22:30
18. Rev. 19:7
19. Matt. 28:19
20. Rev. 22:2
21. Rev. 7:9–12
22. Rev. 19:1
23. Rev. 22:3
24. John 1:1–3
25. Rev. 22:5;
    2 Tim. 2:12
26. 1 Cor. 6:3
27. Rev. 21:2
28. Rev. 21:10–27
29. Dan. 7:14;
    Rev. 11:15
30. 2 Cor. 5:8 NIV
31. John 20:31 NIV

ABOUT MARLENE BAGNULL

During the four and a half years it was 'my turn to care' for my aging mother," says compiler and editor Marlene Bagnull, "I often longed for a book that would reassure me that I was not alone and the God would help me to care for my mother. Thanks to the 108 men and women who have shared their hearts and lives, there is now a book to affirm *you* as you care for your aging parent."

Marlene Bagnull has authored three other books and has written hundreds of articles, stories, devotionals, and poems for Christian periodicals. She is the director of the Greater Philadelphia Christian Writers' Conference and a popular speaker at Christian writers' conferences around the nation.

Marlene and her husband, Paul, make their home in a Philadelphia suburb. Paul is a computer programmer and an avid fisherman. Their oldest daughter, Sharon, is married and lives five minutes away from her parents; their daughter Debbie is a senior at Taylor University; and their son, Robbie, is a high school senior.

Marlene is available to speak about caring for the aging parent if you write to 316 Blanchard Road, Drexel Hill, Pennsylvania 19026.

He will wipe away all tears
from their eyes,
and there shall be no more death,
nor sorrow, nor crying,
nor pain.
All of that has gone forever.

Revelation 21:4 TLB